The Faith Adventure

Lee Hunter

BookLocker
Trenton, Georgia

For over 45 years we have been involved in ministry with Christians living under persecution and oppression. Sometimes it was challenging in the places we traveled, because of the hostility to the Gospel, dangerous travel and sickness. But the blessings, through the people we met, and the miracles we have seen, our faith grew. We give all the glory to God!

It was such a blessing to relive these experiences as I was writing them down. I pray you also, will grow and be strengthened in your relationship with the Lord as you read these adventures.

I want to thank Ron Kohler, Dr. Sam Dronebarger and Jennifer Hall for helping me with their suggestions, encouragement and editing to bring this Faith Adventure to you.
I especially want to thank my wife Pat for all her prayers, support and encouragement all these years.

This book is dedicated to those Christians around the world who experience persecution daily because of their commitment to Jesus Christ.

CONTENTS

IN THE BEGINNING

Acts 13: 2,3 As they ministered to the Lord and fasted, The Holy Spirit said, "Now separate to Me Barnabas and Saul for the work for which I have called them." Then, having fasted and prayed, and laid hands on them, they sent them away.

How did this all begin; this Bible study, faith, smuggling Bibles? In the spring of 1971 I was a junior at the University of Iowa. During the day I attended classes, at night I worked to support my family. I was on a quest for truth. Involved in the anti-war movement of the time, organizing rallies, trying to find meaning unsuccessfully through politics and athletics. Is this an unusual combination!

While in parochial high school I had abandoned traditional religion and belief in a God of religion. A student friend at the University had captured my attention. While waiting for class one day I asked him what made him so different. I could see a specialness about him that I didn't have. He was a good student, good athlete, quick with encouraging words for others. I asked him if he read Dale Carnegie's: "How to Win Friends and Influence People?" He laughed and said no, but he read the Bible a lot. Stunned, I responded in an unkind way: "the Bible was bull…. and a bunch of fairy tales. He didn't get mad, just quietly responded he based his whole life on that book.

Convicted and seeing the reality of "something" in his life, I picked up a Bible and started to look through it. It didn't make much sense to me. Two weeks later I made an appointment to talk with him about it. We met in his dorm room and at his desk while he explained the Gospel to me. He told me things about Jesus I had never known before; about His love, the forgiveness He offered and eternal life available to me by faith. We talked for a long time. He shared a scripture that changed my life. Revelation 3:20 Jesus says: "Behold, I stand at the door (of your heart) and knock. If any man will hear My voice and open the door, I will come into him and sup with him and he with Me." I got up and opened the door to his room and said: "Jesus, I want you to come into my life and forgive my sin." In that moment all the guilt from sin was washed away. I was changed. This began my search for the Source of all Truth. I desired to know Him in a personal and intimate way.

A key concept to growing in faith is what the Bible calls: "Abiding." According to Strong's Exhaustive Concordance the word "abide" is derived from the Greek word: "Meno" which means to: Remain, dwell, endure and persevere. As we look at the scriptures in this book keep this definition in mind.

In our ministry and travels, one problem we see in so many believers is low self-image. Individuals do not understand the relationship the Lord desires to have with His people, or comprehend the power He has made available to us, for competing the task He has given us. Our lives would be so much different if we did. We were saved to fulfill a special role for God that only we could do. He needs you, your worship and your life. He DESIRES a relationship with you as close and intimate as you desire with a spouse or close friend. Is it hard for you to comprehend the God who made the earth, heavens and all its creatures needs you?

There is a new beginning for all of us. We all have a part in God's plan to reach the world with the Gospel. We just need the courage to step out.

FIRST TRIP INTO COMMUNIST EASTERN EUROPE

1Cor. 12:25,26 …there should be no division in the body, but that the members should have the same care for one another. and if one member suffers, all the members suffer with it, if one member is honored, all the members rejoice with it."

My wife, two co-workers and I lumbered along between the West and East German borders. We were traveling in a large self-contained camper. There was a big difference between this camper and others. This one had secret compartments holding hundreds of Russian and Polish Bibles, Christian books and Gospel portions. If we were caught with this material, it meant confiscation of the books, arrest and detainment for us, or worse.

We were aware of others who had tried. Many were successful. Some got caught. A few were arrested. Some went to jail. I wasn't afraid for myself it was only a couple of days ago that I had resolved my fear for my wife. I believed it was better to be in the center of God's perfect will, no matter the cost or circumstances.

Our team leader was driving. She was fluent in Russian and German, and had traveled in these areas before. I was riding in the passenger seat, my wife and other co-worker rode in the back seats. I glanced back at them and noticed a floor panel in the middle of the floor had sprung its lock and buckled the floor boards. I told the team leader to pull off the road. We were in the middle of no man's land. I knew binoculars in the hands of East German border guards had to be watching us. While the two of us tried to fix the compartment, my wife and the other lady grabbed a roll of toilet paper and headed into the tress near our stopping place. I prayed this would divert the border guards. When they returned, we had restored the floor panels to original appearance and drove the rough road to the guard posts. The guards ordered us off the road and began their inspection. While our passports and papers were examined another guard looked over the exterior of the camper. Another guard opened the back door and climbed into the camper. The morning sun flooded into through the door and revealed the floor panel had once again buckled. I turned around in my seat and prayed the Lord would blind the eyes of the guard and direct his steps around the loose floor boards. I was perspiring in spite of the cool September morning. He walked directly on the loose floorboards. I prayed more fervently. He walked around and looked in some of the overhead cabinets where we kept food and canned goods. He smiled, gave us our papers and told us we could leave.

The Lord had just taught me a big lesson in His school of faith. In the days, weeks and years to come, He would teach me more, much more.

Each one of us will have an opportunity to care for others in the Body of Christ. Through our caring we identify with those who suffer

A LESSON IN PRAYER

John 14:6 I Am the way, the truth, and the Life, no-one comes to the Father, except through Me.

My wife and I and two co-workers were scheduled to deliver literature and teaching tapes to a pastor in Central Poland. My wife was to go with the team leader. We had scouted route earlier in the day. I was amazed to see so many Russian soldiers occupying the area. As the ladies completed their disguises, we dropped them off on an empty street under cover of darkness. The other co-worker and I went to a designated parking spot to wait one hour. We then drove back into the city on selected streets, planning on seeing the two ladies, pick them up and be on our way. God's plan was different. We drove as close to the believer's house as we dared. We felt we must have missed them in the dark. We drove all the way back to our parking spot. The ladies weren't there. I was getting concerned. I thought they might be lost, so I drove around and got ourselves lost. My concerns were growing into panic. I imagined them taken into custody by the Russians. What were we to do? I stopped the vehicle and we prayed for direction. After some time, I opened my eyes and felt the Lord leading me to drive to the nearest corner and take a right turn. There they were walking, looking for us. The Lord needed us to wait on Him to give us direction when we were lost.

What does the Bible have to say about all this? For me all of life and truth has its beginning and end in Jesus Christ. Consider the scripture at the top. John 3:16 "For God so loved the world that He gave His only begotten Son, that whoever believes in Him should never perish, but have everlasting life."

Should it be so difficult to believe in this great love God has for us? Has anyone offered to lay down their life for you? What would you think of them for this sacrifice?

The closest experience I had like this happened when myself and two pastors were placed under arrest in North East India. Our native pastor told the authorities he would be our guarantee of not trying to escape. If we did something wrong, he would take our place in jail. We were very moved by his heart and care for us.

Imagine! Jesus whom you didn't know, died out of love for you. If God was willing to do this much to show His love for you, what else might He do?

A TRUE GIFT

John 14:27 "Peace I leave you, My peace I give to you; not as the world gives do I give to you. Let not your heart be troubled, neither let it be afraid."

I was told by a pastor in Havana, Cuba: "When you know the TRUTH, there are no bars, there are no restrictions." Not only was there a need for Bibles in Cuba, they also needed food. Everything is rationed; food, clothing and gasoline.

A coworker and I had gone through customs with a large quantity of Spanish study Bibles for seminary students. On our way to the Bible school, we stopped at a diplomatic store to purchase 50-100 pound sacks of beans and rice. We also bought canned meat and powdered milk. Foreigners and diplomats are allowed in these special stores. Cubans aren't allowed even if they have money. Our vehicle struggled up a steep hill to the Bible school. We had a lot of extra weight. When we arrived, we met with the director and some of the staff and students. They were amazed at all the food we brought them. Some of the people wept. The director picked up one of the Bibles and hugged it. As he waved his hand over the food items he said: "these things are very important to our bodies, but this (waving the Bible) is the best gift of all."

Our opening scriptures are such great words of assurance. Nothing this world has to offer can compare with the peace God has for His people. If the Lord has done all these things for us, why doubt the peace He desires to give us.

I am reminded of the incredible book Norma Grant wrote entitled "Vanya." It is the story of a young Christian in the Russian army. The Lord miraculously sustained the young man in spite of heavy persecution. At one time he was forced to spend entire winter evenings outside his barracks dressed only in his summer uniform. He said he was never cold but was protected in the warm glory of the Lord. His officers could not believe him nor explain how he didn't freeze to death. When his testimony and God's provision impacted the lives of fellow soldiers, he was martyred to silence his witness.

His peace will sustain you in all kinds of circumstances, the good and the difficult. He is waiting.

HUNGER FOR THE WORD OF GOD

Romans 10:17 "So then faith comes by hearing, and hearing by the Word of God."

How can we grow on our relationship with the Lord? We deepen our understanding and knowledge by taking time to hear from the Lord. One way is through His Word. I met a Christian in China who was involved in. Ministering to believers released from prison or labor camps. He helped them settle down with families, find jobs, or whatever they needed. This man literally glowed with his love for the Lord. As we talked about the Bible and faith, he told me (very humbly} how he had memorized the entire New Testament and was now working on the Old Testament. In his own words: "At one time we had no Bibles, but you have been an answer to our prayers by bringing Bibles. The officials may come and take away our Bibles again, but they can never take away what I have hidden in my heart."

Another verse to encourage and give us confidence: Romans 8:1 "There is therefore now no condemnation to those who are in Christ Jesus, who do not walk according to the flesh, but according to the Spirit." If God hasn't convicted us of unconfessed sin, we do not have to receive a lie from the enemy. Satan has many victories because he convinces believers their sin brings great condemnation and we can't possibly be of any benefit to

God. Soon the believer is helpless and sidelined rather than actively involved in God's plan. We need only claim and obey 1John 1:9 "If we confess our sins, He is faithful and just to forgive us our sins and cleanse us from all unrighteousness."

A few years ago I had the privilege of spending time with Norman Grubb. One of the books he wrote was "Reese Howells: Intercessor." He walked so closely to the Lord in attitude of repentance and peace. He didn't just talk a good faith, he lived it. He walked in what he called "continuous revival." His life and writings made a big impact on me. Although well into his eighties he was still a captivating speaker and mighty prayer warrior.

The Lord will bring many circumstances in our lives that will be opportunities to grow in faith. I cannot stress the importance of spending time reading, studying and praying the Word of God.

TRANSFORMED BY REPENTANCE AND PRAYER

John 14:27 Peace I leave with you, My peace I give to you; not as the world gives do I give to you. Let not your heart be troubled, neither let it be afraid.

Is there a magic formula when it comes to "continuous revival?" Do we have to get into some kind of spiritual penalty box when we slip? It is so simple that theologians have complicated the Christian life beyond belief. Simply admit your fault to the Lord and get on with His plan for you. Apply the verses and with the victories begin a new. How much repentance is enough? One hour, one day, a month, a lifetime? The Old Testament repentant offered sacrifices then was forgiven. The New Testament gives us 1John 1:9 "If we confess our sins He is faithful and just to forgive us our sins, and cleanse us from all unrighteousness." While in Hong Kong we met with a former drug addict who worked as a hit man for one of the Hong Kong gangs. He currently works at Jackie Pullinger's camp. Jackie is the author of: "Chasing the Dragon." He had nightmares of his old life. When he finally repented of his crimes, claiming 1John 1:9, he shared how he knew instant forgiveness and the peace that comes with the removal of the guilt of sin. There is peace and rest available to us no matter the circumstances. Will we believe what God has to say to us in our present situation?

TRUE FAITH, TRUE RELIGION

Proverbs 3:5,6 Trust in the Lord with all your heart, and lean not on your own understanding; in all your ways acknowledge Him, and He will direct your paths.

While in Burma we had an opportunity to visit a number of temples. I was impressed by the amount of gold that made up the temple and it's Buddha's. The government could take the gold from one temple and pay off any national debt and feed the people. Another thing was the lack of joy among the followers who came and went through the motions of ritual. There was only the ritual and the deadness of religion and little hope. This is the same government that allows its police and military to force Christians to reject their faith and accept Buddhism. This is done at the point of a gun barrel. Refusal results in very bad things happening.

It isn't necessary to complicate the simplicity of a relationship with our risen Lord. It's quite simple Isn't it? Our body is a temple, inhabited by the Spirit of the living God. We don't need a degree in theology to understand this truth. We only need child-like faith to believe it, and the courage to live it.

I acknowledge my need, my trust in Him; every day, every hour. He will not disappoint!

A MIRACLE IN FAITH

John 15:5,7 I Am the vine, you are the branches. He who abides in Me, and I in him, bears much fruit; for without Me you can do nothing. If you abide in Me, and My words abide in you, you will ask what you desire, and it shall be done for you.

I met the most incredible family from China. I'll call them the Kang family. The second oldest son, Daniel told me of one experience they had when he was 11 years old. His mother, a dynamic house church leader had been arrested. His father was already in prison. His older brother had been beaten to death with bamboo clubs by police officials. His crime was refusing to tell them about other house church pastors his family was involved with. Daniel, his younger brother and sister had been placed in an empty home. Neighbors under threat of prison from the police, were ordered not to feed or care for the children. Daniel said he and his siblings were scared and hungry. They did the only thing they knew how to do. They prayed and asked God to help them. They searched the house only to find a solitary bowl of rice. They thanked the Lord for it then ate their fill. That night they were hungry again. They went to the bowl of rice and found it full again. Daniel said the bowl of rice never ran out the whole time their mother was in prison. That lasted for more than a month. When his mother was released the bowl of rice ran out.

This is the beginning of a life that abides in Christ. First, we understand God's love for us. Next, we accept His dwelling in us. Now we move into trust beyond ourselves to the greatest source of strength, knowledge and truth. Since He indwells us, we have access to Him continually. We don't have to be in a church building or prayer room to know the Lord's presence with us.

THE LORD MEETS US ANYWHERE

Psalm 23:2,3 He makes me lie down in green pastures; He leads me beside still waters. He restores my soul; He leads me in the paths of righteousness for Hs name's sake.

In our travels in access restricted countries, we have been in church services (many of them were secret) in jungles, beaches, attics, forests backyards and city squares. We knew God was with us in each one of these places, as if we were in a nice comfortable pew in the United States.

We met a group of believers in a banana grove in Cuba. These Christians are not allowed to meet anywhere except at designated times in designated church buildings. If the pastor wanted to visit a sick parishioner he would have to get permission from the local police. They would obviously refuse. We were taking a great risk, but it was at the request of our pastor host. We had a wonderful time of fellowship and ministry over the Word. The Lord truly came down in that meeting and brought blessing and encouragement.

Let us again consider another statement by the Apostle Paul in Ephesians 3:17 – "That Christ may dwell in your hearts through faith..." If we have the Lord's presence in us, then anywhere we are is an opportunity for fellowship with the Creator. Jesus said in Mat. 6:33

"But seek first the kingdom of God and His righteousness, and all these things shall be added unto you." Where do we seek Him? In our hearts! Does it have to be an audible prayer? I hope not. I couldn't afford to stop for a prayer service when going through customs in Cuba with my luggage full of Spanish Bibles. But I have great fellowship with His Spirit in my heart. He leads me in the way I need to go. He directs my actions and words. and when He takes me through successfully, He get's all the glory.

The Lord desires our fellowship. Where better than at the source of thought and action which is in our heart.

A FAITH GROWING OPPORTUNITY

Ps. 91:1 "He who dwells in the secret place of the Most High shall abide in the shadow of the Almighty."

In training for courier work with a mission working in Eastern Europe and the Soviet Union, we were not allowed to take our personal Bible or New Testament on a trip behind the Iron Curtain. We had to rely on scriptures we had memorized for strength and encouragement. It was one of the hardest things I had ever done. It was even more challenging for those who had not committed much scripture to memory.

It seems to me the "secret place of the Most High" is right in our hearts. and what a grand place for refuge, "The shadow of the Almighty." What can possibly penetrate that but what the Lord allows? In training others for travel to restricted countries, I've always stressed: Your level of spiritual maturity isn't reflected by the success or failure as a Bible courier, but by your obedience to the Lord. We had a team of six people carrying Bibles into Cuba. All but one had gone through customs uneventfully and were waiting on a tour bus for our last team member to come through. We waited a long time, and some of the other tourists were starting to complain about the wait. They had no idea what we were doing, or that we were from the "States." Eventually one of the co-workers walks out of the customs building, noticeably downcast. There were two armed customs agents with him. They got on the bus, read our names off a list and ordered us off the bus. The agents herded us back into customs and ordered us to open our luggage. They found our Bibles and Christian literature. They began to yell and threaten us. The tour bus left without us. The agents ordered us to unpack our books and turn them over. My wife kept a LARGE purse on the floor apart from her luggage. The customs people wound up taking almost two thirds of our literature. They didn't find what my wife had in her purse or what we carried on our persons. Fortunately, we weren't strip searched. After humiliating us they released us. We found transportation to our hotel.

Some of the team was depressed. I wasn't sure what the others were thinking and I didn't want there to be any brooding. I told the team when we got settled in our rooms, we would have a meeting on the beach out of ear shot of hotel personnel. We had a great time of fellowship, prayer and talking. We focused on the ministry opportunities ahead of us. Taking stock of what we did get through customs was a real blessing. We wanted to see what the Lord would bring out of a "bad situation." Rather than condemn our co-worker, we lifted him up. Anyone can successfully carry Bibles through customs and not get caught. It takes a real spiritual person to get caught and look at the blessings the Lord has in store because of the experience.

We choose to abide in the "secret place" and receive the blessings of His presence in spite of circumstances.

WHY MUST I SUFFER LIKE THIS?

Job 7:20 Have I sinned? What have I done to You, O Watcher of men? Why have You set me as Your target, so that I am a burden to myself?

Why does the Lord allow the things He does in our lives? So many books have been written and messages given on why either good or bad things happen to God's people. Why does my baby have to be sick? Why am I in such bad health? Why would God allow such a good person to die? Why is my boss mean to Me? Why has the Lord allowed such a disaster in my life? Job asked the same thing. How did God answer him? He didn't! He simply revealed a part of His glory to Job, and Job repented and sought forgiveness. Something happens to those who have a visitation of the manifest presence of God. Re-read the book of Job. No one has suffered as much as that man, except Jesus Himself. But the Lord allowed it to gain a victory over Satan. In the end He blessed Job with twice as much as he had before the trial, to show His love and acceptance of Job. God does not reveal His complete plan ahead of time, but as we have seen from the scriptures, He loves us unconditionally. Not like many who put conditions on our love and relationships.

My wife and I had set up a courier program in Hong Kong to help a missions organization. We worked closely with the ministry director to organize living quarters and personnel. A few years later I had a chance to go back and visit the Hong Kong base. The work was going well and many Bibles were getting into China. We traveled with small teams from around the world who desired to carry Bibles into China. Next time I will share about a powerful experience we had on one of those trips.

We all face challenges. Maybe not as severe as Job. But in reading about his trials, we can take comfort in Job's restoration. So let it be so with us.

A MIRACLE IN TRUTH

1John 4:18 There is no fear in love; but perfect love casts out all fear...the one who fears is not perfected in love.

A co-worker and I were approached by staff leaders from a missions organization we were assisting, asking us if we would be willing to carry Bibles through a particular border that a large quantity of Chinese Bibles were being confiscated. This border hadn't been tried in a long time, and they wanted to know if it was still difficult. What they were really asking for is "guinea pigs," so of course we agreed.

We had one other American with us and several bags full of Bibles. We were a part of a large oriental group on a tour bus. We were the only non-Chinese. When we arrived at the border outpost, I had prayed and felt led to leave my bags of Bibles on the bus and go through customs empty handed. The others decided to do the same. We proceeded through the customs check and I waited for the other two to complete their check. It seemed to take an unusual amount of time. Finally, a customs agent ordered us back into the customs building and asked us if we had left any bags on the bus. We answered affirmatively. He said Bibles had been found in those bags and we were under arrest.

Well, this was quite exciting. My first thought was what a great story this would be to tell back home. Uniformed officials escorted us to an interrogation room. Now I wasn't sure what would happen. When we had gone into the room the door was shut and locked. We sat or stood waiting to see what would happen next. After a considerable time, a high-ranking agent came into the room, and closed the door behind him. He asked us why we were carrying Bibles. My friend responded by asking if they were illegal. The agent wanted to know who we were taking them to. He spoke rather gruffly. I make it a habit to carry a tract in the language of the country I'm traveling in. I pulled out a Chinese tract and asked the agent: "Could you please do me a favor? Someone gave this to me and I don't speak Chinese. Could you please tell me what it says?" He replied: "That's the problem with you Americans, you bring literature into this country you can't even read." I said: "That's true but if you read the brochure for me, I will at least know what it says." He was a bit crabby and grabbed it and said: "oh all right I'll read it." I said: "That's great, now what does this first page say, as I pointed to the Chinese characters. He said: "God loves everyone..." I said: "Isn't that great, just like us. We love the Chinese people. What does this page say?" As I opened it for him. He started to read silently, then responded: "No, no this is illegal, we can't be doing this." He pocketed the tract, turned and left the room, closing the door. Now I was really concerned about what was going to happen. Our traveling companion said: "Now you've really done it. We'll never get out of here." As the words left his mouth the door opened and the official waved us out, handed us our passports and told us we could leave. We weren't given our Bibles back but... Let's just say I prayed much for the customs official that interrogated the Americans who couldn't read Chinese.

To fear is to lack faith. Shouldn't we want to choose to remain in His perfect love where no fear dwells?

SURVIVING THE UNTHINKABLE

Romans 8:28 says "and we know all things work together for good to those who love God, to those who are called according to His purpose."

Is Paul only speaking of good things that happen to us? It says: "all things." God loves us so much He blesses us with the privilege to suffer for Him on occasion. Why? So He can be glorified in our lives! I feel Paul is a very good example, or pattern, for the Christian who desires to know God in the most intimate and personal way. We don't have to read what he says, look at his life. Very few have suffered as much as he did. Very few loved the Lord as much as he did, because he gave up everything for Christ. Paul wanted to be obedient and useful to the cause of Christ. No sacrifice was too great.

Pastor Barnabas is an example of one who suffered must for the cause of Christ. He survived the "killing fields" of Cambodia to become one of the leading and most respected ministers. During the war his entire family was taken from the city to do farm work in village areas. When their usefulness wore out, they were killed. I stood on the ground where Barnabas' family and hundreds of thousands of innocents were butchered. In order not to appear as an intellectual, Barnabas threw his glasses away to avoid sudden death. He worked hard on a farm and was brutally treated. When liberation came, he walked back to Phnom Phen to find all of his family gone. He recovered and began an incredible ministry to liberate the people of Cambodia from Shiva, the goddess of war and death. Many people are coming to saving knowledge of Jesus Christ under the ministry of Pastor Barnabas.

It's hard to imagine God's purpose to see so many killed by the Khmer Rouge in Cambodia or the millions of Jews under Hitler. Let's make it our desire to trust Him. Someday all things will be made clear.

PERSEVERING THROUGH ADVERSITY

2Cor. 11:23-28 "Are they ministers of Christ? I speak as a fool– I am more: in labors more abundant, in stripes above measure, in prison more frequently, in death often. From the Jews five times I received forty stripes minus one. Three times I was beaten with rods, once I was stoned, three times I was shipwrecked, a night and a day I have been in the deep, in journeys often, in perils in the city, in perils in the wilderness, in perils in the sea, in perils among false brethren, in weariness and toil, in sleeplessness often, in hunger and thirst, in fastings often, in cold and nakedness– besides the other things, what comes upon me daily, my deep concern for all the churches."

Paul trusted God. Paul knew that God's plan for his life was perfect.

While in Poland we visited Auschwitz death camp. It was an experience that is branded into my memory never to be removed. As we walked around the buildings, seeing displays of rooms full of human hair, the gas chambers and the ovens. To think of all the Jews, Christians and others who were exterminated there was overwhelming. You didn't hear any birds singing, and there was still an unpleasant odor about the place. It was hard to imagine what it must have been like for those who were crammed into tiny cells with no room to sit, lay down or able to breathe. Even in all this horror, the Lord was there, using condemned believers to minister life to other condemned prisoners. Some of the Auschwitz prisoners could identify with the apostle Paul.

Did God use Paul's suffering to minister to others? Did God use suffering prisoners in Auschwitz to minister to others? The Word of God promises it did.

AN ANSWER TO PRAYER

Phil. 1:21 "For me to live is Christ, and to die is gain".

In Paul's letter to the Philippians, we gain insight into this man of God, and his thoughts on life. Paul's circumstances did not dictate his attitude toward God. Paul had an abiding relationship with God that we ought to be praying fervently for. Paul practiced the presence of God continually. Death and life had the same result for Paul; the presence of God.

When I think of circumstances and the presence of the Lord, I recall an experience My wife and I had in Poland. Late one night the two of us were waiting in our camper on a dark street in the eastern part of the country when it was still under communist rule. Two co-workers had been dropped off for a delivery of Bibles to a contact. We had waited some time and were discussing some of the other contacts we would make on this trip. A strong prompting from the Lord came that we should be praying for our friends. There was some kind of trouble so we prayed. Eventually they showed up excited and out of breath. They told us how on their way to deliver the Bibles, a soldier had stepped out from behind a tree and held up his hands to stop them. Then for some reason, his arms dropped to his side, he turned around and walked up the street ignoring them. They quickly ran off to complete the delivery and return to the camper. We realized that the time they were stopped was the same time we were prompted to pray.

I realized as I "die" daily to self, I'm able to "live" more abundantly for Christ. Less of me makes room for more of Christ to perform greater tasks for Him daily.

GOD'S PLANS NOT OURS

Philip. 4:6,7 Be anxious for nothing, but in everything by prayer and supplication with thanksgiving let your requests be made known to God. and the peace of God, which passes all understanding shall guard your hearts and minds in Christ Jesus.

In the book of Philippians 4:6-8 Paul talks about being in prayer about everything, and to meditate on whatever brings a good report, is noble, just, pure, virtuous, or praiseworthy. It didn't matter to Paul if he was in prison talking to his jailor, or preaching to large numbers of people. Whatever his circumstances he wasn't going to worry about it. He knew his Lord would keep him in all circumstances.

This came true for myself and two co-workers when we traveled to Nagaland, a state in N.E. India. In the past the Christians have suffered terribly at the hands of the government and its military. The Nagas are tribal people whose roots and culture came from Mongolia. Prior to the Gospel message coming to them in the late 1800's, the Nagas were headhunters. Some could be found up to the 1970's. Today the Nagas are over 95% Christian. Over 200,000 Naga people have died at the hands of soldiers, their homes and churches burned down, women raped and pastors killed. I heard their story at a missions conference in Thailand in 1997. I was moved by the Lord to try and minister to their need. The next year with my two co-workers we made arrangements to go to Nagaland. We thought our restricted area permits had been arranged. When we arrived at the airport, we found out there was a conflict with the police and government authorities who had to give us permission to enter the area. We had not received the necessary permits. We were placed under house arrest and taken to a hotel room. We were confined and not allowed to leave until the situation was resolved. Our status seemed to change by the hour. We were informed we may be taken to the border, dropped off and make our way to Calcutta. Another time we were told we may have to go to prison. This was not a pleasant thought. We spent a lot of time praying and reading the Word.

We had been invited to be guest lecturers at the local Bible School and preach in a large crusade. Here we were stuck in our rooms not knowing what was going to happen.

After three days we were allowed some limited freedom, to teach at the Bible school and spend one day at the crusade. We were under constant watch by officials to make sure we wouldn't try to escape. They also reported to their leaders everything we said and did. So the Gospel reached some high Indian officials.

This was an experience to train us to rest totally in the Lord in spite of the circumstances. Like Paul might say: "What a blessed way to live."

I pray we can all learn to look beyond our present circumstances, knowing God has a higher purpose.

IN MINISTERING TO OTHERS
WE ARE BLESSED

Philip. 4:11-13 "Not that I speak in regard to need, for I have learned in whatever state I am, to be content. I know how to be abased, and I know how to abound. Everywhere and in all things, I have learned both to be full and to be hungry, both to abound and to suffer need. I can do all things through Christ who strengthens me."

What is our attitude and the pattern we use for our lives? Maybe attitude is the wrong word to use here. How about way of life! When we grow in faith by abiding in Christ, we leave the worrying to Him. He sees the end of His plan for us from the beginning, The best thing we can do is to trust Him and rest in His presence.

My co-worker and I had traveled a long way in our little car. From Holland, through both Germanys, Hungary to the Romanian border. We had dropped off some literature to a pastor contact in Hungary and had an opportunity for some ministry in a small church. We were now on our way to one of the most difficult border crossings in Eastern Europe. We carried some supplies which would be sold on the black market to help a pastor and his family who were experiencing some tough times. Our plan was to stop at a rest area prior to the border. There we would destroy our notes on names and addresses of contacts, and try to hide our supplies the best we could. As can happen sometimes, we got lost and having problems reading our map. I was trusting my co-workers map reading skills to get us on track. The Lord had a different plan. We came around a bend in the road to find the Romanian border crossing. We couldn't stop and back up without drawing suspicion. We took deep breaths, prayed and drove up to the crossing. I knew the customs people would find our notes, but I prayed the Lord would blind their eyes to what I had written on the pages. These officers spoke excellent English. They searched our car but didn't bother to question us about our supplies. But they did find my notebook with our contacts information. The agent thumbed through the notebook coming to the section where the names of our friends was written. Would we be arrested, beaten, jailed, denied entry? This agent hardly gave it a second look. After checking our passports and visas, they returned my notebook, opened the gate and let us into Romania. When we got out of earshot of the border we lifted all kinds of praise and thanksgiving to the Lord.

Today, can we make the same declaration as the Apostle Paul? Can we believe that Christ will give us the strength to do all He desires us to do?

WHY DO I SUFFER LIKE THIS?

Hebrews 4:9-11 "There remains therefore a rest for the people of God. For he who has entered His rest has himself also ceased from his works as God did from His. Let us therefore be diligent to enter that rest, lest anyone fall after the same example of disobedience." Paul didn't want to be anxious about his abiding in Christ, he wanted to rest in Christ.

My team and I were on a flight from Phnom Pehn, Cambodia, to Ho Chi Minh City, Vietnam. I was battling a major migraine headache and could barely think, let alone pray with good focus. In our luggage we had Bibles for pastors in the city formerly called Saigon. I had been there several times before. The previous year we had all been caught and our Bibles confiscated. At this point I was so sick I didn't care. It would have been alright for them to put me out of my misery. The little Air Cambodia prop plane didn't help. We were bouncing all over the sky because of turbulence. I thanked the Lord when we landed and asked Him to work a miracle to get us and our Bibles through customs. There were six of us on the team. We had split up going through customs so as not to bunch up in case one person was caught. We were the only flight of passengers in the terminal. The customs agents would be in no hurry. As my suitcase full of Bibles, started it's trek on the conveyor to the x-ray machine I prayed the

Lord would divert the attention of the agent watching the x-ray machine so he wouldn't see what was inside my suitcase. As the case entered the machine there was a large crash of metal in the terminal. At that very moment the guard looked up and behind him to see what the noise was about. The conveyor hadn't stopped. In that short amount of time my case went past his screen. I couldn't wait to grab the bag as it came out the other side, and hustle out of the terminal avoid being called back. The other team members also got through safely.

When we are faced with challenging or difficult circumstances, will we choose to be at rest in His purpose, or be filled with anxiety, fear and stress?

THE POWER OF THE
SPIRIT'S LEADING

Psalm 37:7,8 "Rest in the Lord, and wait patiently for Him; do not fret because of him who prospers in his way, because of the man who brings wicked schemes to pass. Cease from anger, and forsake wrath; do not fret, it only causes harm." The sweet Psalmist of Israel has some encouraging words on the topic of rest. Such wise words from a man who abided in His God, and whom God referred to as His friend.

The Lord puts us in situations to show us our level of rest in Him. When Poland was still under communist domination, a co-worker and I had an assignment to deliver Russian Bibles to a church that had a ministry to Russian soldiers and their families. We only had the name out our pastor contact, and the church was large with a number of pastors. One has to be careful when asking questions even among church people in a restricted country.

We arrived at the church after a large evening service. We wanted to be careful and not draw a lot of attention to ourselves, so we prayed and asked the Lord to direct us to the right individual. As we walked to the steps of the church my eyes were drawn to a man, and I felt he was the one we were to meet. My co-worker spoke fluent Russian and German, so we asked him a few questions in Russian. He turned out to be the man we were looking for. We were able to bless their ministry with a large quantity of Russian Bibles they desperately needed.

Can you believe God is working out the circumstances of your life for His greater glory? Believe it!

YES! THE LORD HAS A
SENSE OF HUMOR

Matthew 11:28-30. "Come to me, all you who labor and are heavy laden, and I will give you rest. Take my yoke and learn from Me, for I am gentle and lowly in heart, and you will find rest for your souls. For my yoke is easy and burden is light."

Jesus tells us that He is the source of rest, as well as our example. How else can we learn from Christ, except through what we read in the Bible, or experience in our hearts in an abiding relationship.

Two co-workers and I were going to deliver Bibles in a large city of Burma, (now called Myanmar) to pastors in several different churches. In our briefing we were told to place our underwear on top of our packages of Bibles, because Buddhists would not touch them. I was quite excited at this prospect. In order to help the Lord I decided to put two weeks of dirty underwear on top of my packages. I was sure this would deter any searches by Buddhist customs officials.

When we arrived in the baggage check of customs in the Rangoon airport, I almost had a smirk on my face thinking how quickly I was going to get through customs. I wasn't really surprised when the customs official who assisted me, asked me to open my luggage for inspection. I laughed to myself. My laugh turned to shock when he pushed aside my underwear, picked up one of my packages, waved it in my face and asked me what I had in here. I honestly answered: "Books!" He tore open one of the packages and began to scan the "book." I prayed what he read would not register in his mind. After his search he tossed the Bible on my underwear and told me I was allowed to pass through. The Lord certainly has a since of humor. I realized I was not at a great level of "rest!"

We will have many opportunities in life to test our place of rest in the Lord. I don't look at falling short as a sign of failure. More like a reminder to grow in faith and trust.

GREAT HUNGER FOR
THE WORD OF GOD

Psalm 31:20 "You shall hide them in the secret place of Your presence from the plots of man; you shall keep them secretly in a pavilion from the strife of tongues."

God is our source of strength, wisdom, protection, guidance and action. He is our shield, and His Word our weapon in spiritual warfare. God told Moses His name was I AM. Jesus in the New Testament referred to Himself as I AM. He tells those who abide in Him: "I AM; whatever My people need." Should we need any of these things mentioned earlier in this paragraph, He is the source and provider of it all.

A pastor friend from where I live developed a "Sister Church" relationship to a small church in Havana, Cuba. Among their many needs was a keyboard. Their piano was broken and warped. On our next trip to the island we were going to meet that need and many others.

When we got to Cuba we went to a diplomatic store. This is a market that could not be used by Cubans, only by foreigners. We purchased a keyboard and some food items the pastor and his congregation could not get on their own. Rationing of food and clothing was a real problem. We delivered the keyboard and other "gifts" to the pastor and his family. They invited us to stay and take part in the evening service and bring words of encouragement.

At the close of the service which was attended by civilians and military people from a nearby base, we invited people who would like a scripture copy to come forward and get one. They were colorful and easy to read in Spanish. There was no order to the chaos that followed. The congregation pushed, shoved and ran forward to get a copy of the Word. I'd never seen anything like it. The pastor was concerned we would be offended and said: "Scriptures are very hard to come by here, and when they are it is very expensive." We were NOT offended, just desirous that we had more to give. Eventually the whole village had come through and got a copy of the precious book. We were blessed to be an answer to these peoples need.

Why does the Lord want to hide you in the secret place of His presence? It may be to reveal to you His love and care for every area of your life.

GOD SPEAKS IN SIMPLE WAYS

John 15:1-7 "I am the vine, My Father is the vinedresser. Every branch in Me that does not bear fruit He takes away; and every branch that bears fruit He prunes, that it may bear more fruit. You are clean already because of the word which I have spoken to you: Abide in Me, and I in you. As the branch cannot bear fruit of itself, unless it abides in the vine, neither can you unless you abide in Me... He who abides in Me and I in him, bears much fruit, for without me you can do nothing. If anyone does not abide in Me, he is cast out as a branch and is withered, and they gather them and throw them into the fire, and they are burned. If you abide in Me and My words abide in you, you will ask what you desire, and it will be done for you. By this My Father is glorified, that you bear much fruit; so you will be My disciples. As the Father loved Me, I also have loved you, abide in My love. If you keep My commandments you will abide in My love, just as I have kept My Father's commandments and abide in His love. These things I have spoken to you, that My joy may remain in you, and that your joy may be full. This is My commandment, that you love one another as I have loved you. Greater love has no man than this, than to lay down one's life for his friends. You are My friends if you do whatever I command you. No longer do I call you servants... but I have called you friends, for all things I have heard from My Father I have made known to you. You did not choose Me, but I have chosen you, and appointed you, that you should go and bear fruit, and that your fruit should remain, that whatever you ask the Father in My name He may give you. These things I have commanded you, that you love one another."

I am particularly fond of Jesus' words on abiding in Him. You may have read them many times before, but when considered prayerfully, they take on a new meaning for you, based on your current knowledge of God's desire for you.

I compare what Jesus says about abiding and pruning to apple trees we had in our yard when I was growing up. The branches in the apple tree did not object or struggle against being a part of the tree. The life -giving sap was drawn up through the roots into the trunk and flowed out to the branches. The branches did what was natural to them. As they received the sap, they would grow, bud, then flower. In time the flowers gave way to tiny apple sprouts. In the Fall we were able to pick nice ripe apples for snacking, canning or giving away to others. Every few years we had to prune some branches. The branches did not rebel or draw back. It never failed to produce outstanding apples when branches were pruned. I learned something else. When the branches were pruned the trees withstood storms much better. If they had been left to grow on their own, the branches would become too long and blown off large sections of the trunk, rather than a few flowers or small twigs. In dry years, the roots of the trees were forced to grow deeper into the ground to seek moisture. This strengthened the foundation, and the trees held up against the storms. Through all this, the branches had to do nothing but rest in the trunk, or as we have been saying, the branches abided in the tree.

Difficult times will come to us all. Not to punish us or hurt us, but to make us stronger for the marathon run of life.

THE IMPARTING OF A SPIRITUAL GIFT

Rom. 1:11,12 I long to see you that I may impart to you some spiritual gift to make you strong. That is, that you and I may be mutually encouraged by each others faith.

I pray you can understand the relationship the Lord desires with each of His children. The fruit of the apple trees we grew in our yard blessed us with nourishment and health. We always had enough to share with others. It is much like the life of the saint who abides in Christ. Our fruit will bless others. They see our life and are encouraged to do the same. The Body of Christ is exhorted, encouraged, and built up. The needs of the saints are met, and souls are added to the kingdom.

A fascinating experience about the growing of the kingdom occurred when a co-worker and I were on a small island in the South China Sea in Southeast East China We had delivered some Bibles to some house church pastors, and decided to do a little sight seeing. We found a church that had been closed and locked up. We were looking around to find a way in. A lady we assumed was the caretaker came and though she spoke no English, unlocked a door and let us go inside. The church had not been used in a long time. Dust was thick everywhere. We went through the motions of looking around. I then felt led to take out one of my trusty tracts I carry with me in the native language.

I motioned the lady to take it and read through it. As she slowly read it tears came to her eyes. When she finished reading she folded her hands in prayer, weeping. She looked around the church, pointed to the cross, then pointed to her heart. Tears came to my eyes. Before we left we gave her a New Testament. She bowed several times. I believe she was thankful.

What a blessing for me to impart to others a spiritual gift - which is the Word of God. To encourage another and have her encourage me in faith. Try it yourself. It's so uplifting.

COME TO THE LIGHT

John 1:5 The Light shines in the darkness, and darkness has not overcome it.

I had books sitting on my shelf about a missionary to Calcutta, India named Mark Buntain. I'd never read them. In March 2000, two pastors and I visited Mission of Mercy in Calcutta, on our way to N.E. India. Mark Buntain founded this outreach in the 1950's. We were told by the current director: "Calcutta has been called the city of the dreadful night, an out-post of hell, the cholera capital of the world, city of the living dead, armpit of the world, and such tragic names. I call it the city God loves and Jesus died for. Buntain had been told by his mission board that his vision for Calcutta was not theirs. But this praying man of God had been given a mandate by God. In spite of all that came against him from the Christian and secular community, he pursued his vision. Today Mission of Mercy feeds over 30,000 people a day, a modern 180 bed hospital with top notch staff and equipment, nursing school, Bible school with over 100 students, high school for 1300 students, a church that seats 1500 people. Mission of Mercy is recognized and respected by the government of India. We were blessed to take part in the feeding program. Going in a large truck to villages outside the city. There we provided the only food these villagers would receive this day. We also shared in the mission school with eager young students. Many of these children were from families who were "rag pickers." Parents and children who spent their days in the city dump scrounging for anything they can pick up and resell. Even small scraps of cloth tossed out by someone else. Mission of Mercy has worked closely with Mother Theresa's Sisters of Mercy on many projects. This man's vision and heart has certainly been attractive and appealing to others. By the way, I found those books on my shelf and read them and was blessed even more.

Do you have a friend or relative who seems to be lost in the darkest place? Your light will shine in the darkest places. Let it shine!

COUNTING THE COST OF FOLLOWING JESUS

2Tim. 3:12 Indeed, all who desire to live a Godly life in Christ Jesus will be persecuted.

There is no fear in laying down ones life for another, because it is no longer you who lives, but Christ who lives in you. This abiding relationship isn't nurtured in the hurry-up world of today, which only produces fruit of anxiety, fear and stress. It is nurtured by a turning inward to the indwelling One. He abides in the quiet and rest of heart, and there we will meet Him.

In 1999 a House Church pastor I knew of in Central China who had a deep abiding relationship with the Lord. He was arrested and threatened with prison, and worse, if he did not close down his House Church. He refused all the threats and intimidation. Finally, he was taken to the village center by police officials. Villagers were ordered to urinate in a horse trough. When there was enough urine filling the through the officials drowned the pastor in it.

Do you desire to live a Godly life in Christ Jesus? Expect to be challenged even to the point of persecution. Remember Jesus Christ is with you.

HUMOR IN CHALLANEGING CIRCUMSTANCES

Romans 8:28 and we know that those who love God all things work together for good, for those who are called according to His purpose.

A coworker, my wife and I were in a campground in Transylvania, Romania. We had arrived earlier in the day to make arrangements for a delivery of Bibles to a pastor contact. Our co-worker had driven to the pastor's house while my wife and I set up camp. On his return we decided to unload the materials from the secret compartment in the camper and place them in large bags for the delivery. We had opened one compartment and had pulled out a large quantity of Bibles, trying to get them packed when a knock came on the door of the camper. We froze! I motioned for our co-worker to answer the door and take care of whoever it was. He squeezed himself into the doorway so when he opened the door no one could see in. When he opened the door and I heard a male voice say loudly: "Come with me!" I didn't know if it was the police, camp officials or what. He stepped out of the camper, being careful to obstruct the vision of our unwanted visitors. When we heard them walk away, I looked at my wife and we knew we had to work quickly to get the Bibles packed up and seal the compartments. It would be much worse for us if our camper was found with built in hiding places. We could be accused of drug smuggling. The penalty would be the same.

We waited and prayed, and no one came. We had no idea what had happened to our friend. We went outside and tried nonchalantly to look around the area and keep the camper in sight. Time was running out, and we decided to leave without him in order to deliver the Bibles on time.

As we prepared to leave, a shout came from the woods about 100 yards from our camp. Here came our friend, running and stumbling to catch us. When he arrived, his speech was slurred and he smelled like a brewery. Waving my hands in front of my face I asked him what had happened. He detailed how a young man who was a college student, saw us set up camp. He found out we were Americans, and wanted to invite us to a party they were having in the woods. He felt it would be best for him to go, rather than arouse suspicion by refusing not to. When he got to their camp fire, they had a huge bottle of wine, and tried to get him to drink some. He felt the sociable thing to do was have a tiny bit then excuse himself. The little bit turned out to be several large tumblers. When the others had drank their fill, he slipped away, because he didn't want to miss the delivery.

When we left in our car, I encouraged our co-worker not to speak or breathe on the pastor or his family. Interesting thing about this. Earlier in the day he and my wife were discussing not compromising beliefs. Jan said he would never drink. My wife said: "Sometimes the Lord puts us in a position that will test us in some area like this." He was still insistent he would never drink. You never know about things, do you?

Do you feel exercising your faiths leading you down a slippery slope? Maybe you're just on the verge of a spiritual breakthrough. Stay focused on Jesus and not on your circumstances.

THE MYSTERY OF HOW
GOD LEADS US

Jeremiah 29:11-13 "For I know the plans I have for you, says the Lord. They are plans for good and not for evil. To give a future and a hope. In those days when you pray, I will listen. You will find Me when you seek Me, if you look in earnest."

God knows the plans He has for us, and will sometimes go to extremes to accomplish it. This was proven to me on a trip into Vietnam. two others and I had a meeting with a lay leader of a church in a large city. We were invited to a meal with a number of key pastors in the area. During the course of the meal a young man knocked on the door and was brought to the dinner table. He stared open mouthed at my companions and me. He excitedly began to relate his experience.

He had walked from the central highlands, a hike of several days. What he related revealed the hand of the Lord. He had been praying for Bibles and Christian literature for the churches he was responsible for. The Lord had spoken to him, and told him he must go to Saigon, and he would get Bibles. He did not believe he had really heard from God this way. So he ignored the Word. But God had other plans for him. He struck the young pastor with a case of malaria., and the only place he could get treatment was in Saigon. Feverish and weak he began the dangerous trek through the jungle.

As he walked the Lord spoke to him again and told him where to go specifically in order to get the Bibles. It was the house we were at. The Lord told him three white people from the West would help him.

When he arrived at the clinic in Saigon, it was closed, so he decided to go to the house the Lord had told him about. When he arrived there, he met us; three white guys from the West. He was very blessed. So were we. So were all those who were eating at the table. Before the young pastor left, we prayed for him, for healing from the malaria. We loaded him down with several bags full of Bibles.

The next day our dinner host picked us up at our hotel, to take us to another appointment. We asked about the well being of the young pastor. She related to us she had seen him earlier in the morning. He had been healed and was hiking back to his village in the highlands, rejoicing and thanking God for the miracles He provides.

Are you wondering if God really has "plans" for you? Ask God to show you His plans. Next, step outside your comfort zone. Do something for the Lord that is beyond your abilities. Watch Him work through you. He will!

GOD DOES WORK IN
MYSTERIOUS WAYS

1Cor. 2:16 For who has known the mind of the Lord, that he should instruct Him? But we have the mind of Christ.

One time I took two ladies from New Zealand into China. We went from Hong Kong to our port in China by hover craft, which was an experience by itself. As is our habit, we separated in customs to go through passport and luggage check. The Lord worked wonderfully allowing me to get through with my bags of Bibles. I left the customs building and walked a block away, but where I could still see the customs building. I waited for what seemed like a very long time. I knew in my heart the ladies had been caught. But I wanted to wait for them to encourage them. The next thing I saw was two armed officials burst out of the doors of the building. I knew they were looking for me. I prayed hastily asking for the Lord's direction and protection. At that moment a pedicab rolled by me.

I didn't shout, but walked quickly along-side the pedicab and motioned to the driver I wanted a ride. He stopped, I got money out of my pocket and waved it at him with one hand and waved for him to move quickly with the other. I looked behind me to see the two guards, one hand on hip and the other holding their rifle in the other, looking up and down the streets. The ladies and I had a prearranged hotel we would meet at for just this kind of occasion. The pedicab took me there where I waited in the lobby. They arrived within a couple of hours. They were disappointed but not as disappointed as the guards who let me get away. The ladies said the Chinese officials were very agitated when they returned to the customs area. We went outside where we couldn't be overheard, and had a time of prayer and thanksgiving for what the Lord had accomplished for us. We divided the Bibles I had and delivered them to their destination.

Did you ever pray and think God did not answer your prayer? Maybe God did answer, just not the way you expected. My two friends from New Zealand were caught and had Bibles taken. God knew this would happen, for this was one of those times when "all things work together for good." We trusted god had a greater plan. Maybe God has answered your prayer in a better way than you planned.

HUNGER FOR THE WORD OF GOD

1 Corinth. 3:5 – "Who then is Paul, and who is Apollos, but ministers through whom you believed, as the Lord gave each one? I planted, Apollos watered, but God gave the increase. So then, neither he who plants is anything, nor he who watered, but God gives the increase. Now he who plants and he who waters are one, and each one will receive his own reward according to his own labor.

The Lord allowed us to safely get a large quantity of scriptures through customs. We delivered them without incident to a seminary in Havana, Cuba. Now we had been invited to minister in a house church meeting. We thought there would be a few people gathered around someone's kitchen table for a Bible study. We were surprised to find a lot of people milling around the yard of our hosts. When we entered the house, it was packed full of people. There were no chairs or furniture. Standing room only. The few fans that were running barely succeeded in moving the hot, muggy air. People were in adjoining rooms. They couldn't see, but they could hear. There were people leaning in every ground floor window. The crowd filled the yard area, and spilled out onto the sidewalk. Every one of these people risked questioning and arrest by the authorities for attending an illegal gathering. They didn't care. They wanted to hear the Word of God. My co-worker and I were humbled and impressed by the devotion of these people. The Lord blessed with a Word that ministered mightily in the lives of these people who wanted the Lord to give them direction in their lives.

You say God has not given you the ministry to share your faith with the crowds. That's fine! Maybe God wants you to be a "planter," or a "waterer." Ask God what He has gifted you to do. Then do it. You will receive your "reward" just for using your gifts.

ONE MILLION BIBLES TO CHINA

1Kings 8:61 and may your hearts be fully committed to the Lord our God, to live by His decrees and obey His commands, as at this time.

In the early 1980's, my wife and I were on staff of the ministry of Brother Andrew, the author of "God's Smuggler." Open Doors was involved in a top-secret project to deliver one million Bibles to the House Church of China. We were involved as fund raisers and prayer coordinators. This was an incredible undertaking. The details of "Project Pearl," the name given to this operation, are detailed in a book co-authored by Brother David entitled "Pearl."

The Lord was sought at the birth of Project Pearl, through its completion in the summer of 1981. What impressed me most was the commitment of the crew involved. They had to train secretly, not even their families were privy to the details. When the tug boat and specially built barge that were used to deliver the precious cargo, left the harbor, none of that crew knew if they were going to come back. But they had made the ultimate sacrifice. They were willing to lay down their lives for someone else.

The Lord worked miracle after miracle for the crew and the cargo. The Bibles were delivered, and the crew was able to safely return to patient and praying families. They survived Chinese gun boats, the Chinese Air Force and a typhoon. But this operation greatly impacted the House Church in China. The country would never be the same again. Still today the need for Bibles in China cannot be met. There are printing presses, controlled by the government, which prints and sells Bibles to Christians and churches which are willing to be registered with the government. But there are over 100 million believers who will not be registered and controlled by China's Three Self, government managed church. These Christians need Bibles, study books and our prayers. What will we do? What will you do?

Does your prayer requests seem to be stretching your faith beyond your "commitment?" If God will send one million Bibles to the House Church in China, stay committed to prayer. Surely your prayer request is not too big for God to answer.

SURRENDERING TO THE LORD'S CARE

1Peter 4:12,13 Dear friends, do not be surprised at the fiery ordeal that has come on you to test you, as though something strange were happening to you. But rejoice inasmuch as you participate in the sufferings of Christ, so you may be overjoyed when His glory is revealed.

I so admire the servanthood and humility of my friend, Pastor Phan from Laos. He spent considerable time in a labor camp because of his Christian activities. For a full year and a half, he was in solitary confinement, in stocks. He was allowed one hour a day out of stocks, but still unable to make contact with other prisoners. In his "free time" he had to clean his bamboo tube in which he had to defecate and urinate. He was given very little food in an effort to break his spirit. His wife had been arrested at the same time he was, and for the time he was in the camp, he didn't know of her condition. On top of all this, he was beaten regularly by the guards. When his internment was completed, he was kicked out of Laos. He now lives and works with a ministry in Thailand. Although unable to go back himself, under threat of death, he still ministers through those he trains to go to Laos with Bibles and training books and seminars. It's hard to imagine a man so full of joy and the Holy Ghost, could have suffered so much. Yet he is a dynamic leader. Not in poise, education, or position, but by the power of the Spirit.

We will continue this discussion on leadership and servanthood in the next post. Are you having to endure a "fiery ordeal" right now? Maybe it's physical? Maybe it's emotional? It may even feel overwhelming. Do not give up for your faithfulness will overjoy you "when His glory is revealed."

PRAYING FOR OTHERS TO STAND STRONG

Proverbs 22:4 The reward for humility and fear of the Lord is riches and honor and life.

While we were in Poland, my wife and I met with a remarkable man, Pastor Borda. He had spent three years in prison for working with young people, training them in the Bible, teaching discipleship and prayer. We delivered a large quantity of Bibles and literature he needed in his ministry. Since his release from prison, he continued his work with young people and teenagers. They would come from all over Eastern Europe to his compound for encouragement and training then go back to their countries to win others to the Lord.

As we enjoyed a meal together, I asked him about prayer. What was he praying for? Less restriction from the authorities? More freedom to work with young people? More literature for his work? Or would he like to live in a country with less oppressiveness toward Christians? He said: "No! I am praying for YOU. That America will not become fat from materialism, and turn their back on God."

I was shocked. Up until that time I had never been arrested for my faith. I had never been in prison for practicing my beliefs. I had all the books and teaching tapes I wanted, and he is praying for ME? At first, I was indignant, then I realized the power and truth in his prayer.

Materialism is a real threat to the Body of Christ. Later I thanked him for his comments and prayers.

Are you asking the Lord to show you "humility and fear of the Lord?" His response will be eternal "riches and honor and life." You may lack material wealth but like my friend Pastor Borda you will finish the race with Spiritual wealth that does not perish.

DOING ACTIVITY GOD'S WAY

Isaiah 55:8,9 For my thoughts are not your thoughts, neither are your ways My ways, declares the Lord.

We met with some pastors in Cuba who wanted to put on a conference and invite pastors from all over the Island. They had permission, if they had the finances to get the job done. We couldn't just give them the money to put the conference on. The authorities would want to know where the money came from. We asked them how we could help and not endanger them. The pastors suggested we buy a large tape player (boombox) at the diplomatic store and make a gift of it to them. The Cuban people were not allowed in the diplomatic store. Only tourists and diplomats were allowed to shop and make purchases there. This store had many items of food, clothing and all kinds of items the Cuban people were not allowed to get. Sort of like a small Wall Mart. We didn't understand how it would all work, but we cooperated. They were able to sell the boombox on the black market and have enough money to pay for all the pastors to come to Havana for the conference. It was a great success. If we had balked at the process they suggested for providing the funds, we would have missed an opportunity to be a blessing, and being blessed by the pastors.

Does God's response to your prayer needs ever confuse you? Good! Are you not better off being led by

God's thoughts than yours? Keep praying! God will get you to His intended destination. That's if you let Him lead the way.

STANDING STRONG FOR THE TRUTH

2Tim. 2:12 If we deny Him, He also will deny us.

One of the greatest servants I have ever met was Pastor Lamb from Canton (Guangshou) China. We met him at his house church. He has entertained some of the biggest names in Christianity to visit China. Billy Graham has been with him on one of his trips to China. Many years ago, Pastor Lamb had been arrested and imprisoned for the sake of the Gospel. He was told by prison officials he would be released as soon as he promised to quit teaching and preaching about Jesus. He told us, prison was very hard and he was weak. He gave the prison officials what they wanted and he was quickly released.

He was miserable and heartbroken at what he had done. He went back to the prison and told the officials he took back all he had said to them, and would not deny Jesus, or quit teaching or preaching in His name. He was imprisoned for over 20 years."

Are you struggling? Ready to give up? Trust Jesus! Never "deny" Him. He will never give up on you. He will never "deny" you.

THE BLESSING OF SERVANTHOOD

1Peter 3:14 But even if you should suffer for what is right you are blessed. Do not fear what they fear; do not be frightened.

Another mighty example of servanthood comes from China. A family I met have a powerful story to tell. Mama Kwong sat in her prison cell in great distress and mourning. She had just seen her oldest son beaten to death by soldiers, because she refused to reveal her contacts in the House Church movement, and where she got Bibles to give to believers. She had been an active minister in China's House Churches. Her husband had been in prison for many years. Now this happened to her son. As the soldiers beat him, he begged his mother not to answer their questions concerning her activities with the House Churches. He went to be with Jesus shortly after that. She didn't know what had happened to her other three children when they took her away. (God would miraculously care for them while she was in prison.) This was the third time she had been arrested. Things would not go well for her. Now she cried out to God for strength and help.

She looked around her filthy, smelly cell, praying the Lord to give her direction on what she should do. The Lord began to speak to her heart about the conditions she and the other women prisoners were in. She asked to see the warden of the prison. When the warden granted her an audience, he was shocked at her request to go around and clean each of the cells. He didn't understand why anyone would want to do such a despicable job. But he was more than pleased to allow her to clean the prison.

She was given a bucket, water, soap and a brush. In the first cell the prisoners mocked and kicked at her. In a humble quiet spirit, she sang gospel songs and spoke out scripture she had memorized. Soon the taunts and abuse turned to silence then tears as she shared her testimony with them, all the while cleaning the cell. She led many of those ladies to a relationship with Jesus. And so she did in each one of those filthy cells, day after day. Many women were won to the Lord because of the servants heart revealed in Mama Kwong. Nearly a month after her arrest she was released from the prison. She was reunited with her family. Today they live in Southern California where Mama pastors a Chinese church. In the future I will share some other miracles that occurred with this family.

Are you or your family members suffering one attack after another? Hold on to faith. A "blessing" is coming.

PERSEVERING IN THE
FACE OF OPPOSITION

James I:2,3 Consider it pure joy, my brothers and sisters, whenever you face trials of many kinds, because you know that the testing of your faith produces perseverance.

Real ministry is in serving others, being a help to others. Jesus taught in Mark 10:42-45 "As you know, the kings and great men of the earth lord it over the people; but among you it is different. Whoever wants to be great among you must be your servant. and whoever wants to be greatest of all must be slave of all."

Our servanthood to God is to be expressed through our serving our fellow men. I remember traveling in Eastern Europe, and hearing out of the Soviet Union what gave a pastor credibility to his congregation. It wasn't the number of diplomas on his office wall, or where he went to Bible school or seminary that gave him respect in the eyes of his people. It was the number of years he had spent in labor camps or prison for the cause of Christ that counted to them. The severe trials they experienced and their total dependance on God, prepared them to serve God's people with great authority.

Are you facing "trials of many kinds" right now? Persevere! Why? Because greater strength to "persevere" will follow.

HUMILITY IN SERVING OTHERS

Luke 14:11 For everyone who exalts himself will be humbled, and he who humbles himself will be exalted.

Our New Zealand friend, Eddie, who has done much great ministry in Asia, shared this illustration on being a servant. If two mountain goats meet on a narrow mountain trail, they have few choices. They could butt heads until one or both falls over the edge. They could try to squeeze by each other, which would be impossible on this particular trail, because it is too narrow. The other choice would be for one of them to lay down and allow the other to walk over him. They would both be spared, and the humility would be at a minimum. From our point of view, which one would have the greater blessing, the one who laid down, or the one who walked over the other who willingly laid down?

Have you reached an impasse in a relationship? Maybe it's time to reach out in humility. "Thank you Lord for God will next "exalt" you.

WAITING ON THE LORD
FOR HIS TIMING

Proverbs 17:22 A joyful heart is good medicine, But a crushed spirit dries up the bones.

It is humbling to know God has planned every day of our lives. Psalm 139:16 "You saw me before I was born and scheduled each day of my life before I began to breathe. Every day was recorded in your book." We are here together by divine appointment. We are serving Jesus where ever we are, by divine plan.

After my wife and I came back from our first trip to Eastern Europe. I knew I wanted to work in this type of ministry full time. I applied for work with a ministry in Eastern Europe and the Soviet Union. They had no staff needs at the time. Besides, staff had to raise their own support for income. There were no salaries. I became frustrated, and it showed in my work and in my relationships. Frustration was making an effort to grow into bitterness and anger. This was not a good testimony. During a late -night shift, with no-one around, The Lord got a hold of my heart. Under great conviction, I confessed my sin to Him who forgives. I determined to apologize to my wife and others I dealt with on a daily basis. I sincerely told the Lord: "If you want me to work this job for the rest of my life, I'll do it. I'll do it gladly, and no one will be a better and more productive employee than I." My whole attitude changed. The joy and excitement returned. I went about and did my job like it was all brand new.

Interesting enough, a few months later, another Missions organization who also labored in restricted countries of the world, was going to have a fund -raising meeting in my home area. We volunteered to assist and made some new relationships. We maintained contact, financially supported the work of this ministry, prayed for them and the people they served. Through a series of events, I was offered a job with salary and benefits. We were overjoyed and blessed. Now we would be getting paid to minister to persecuted Christians. It was like a dream come true.

OBEDIENCE TO HIS PLAN

God does have a plan for our lives. Jeremiah 29:11-13 "For I know the plans I have for you, says the Lord. They are plans for good and not for evil. To give a future and a hope. In those days when you pray, I will listen. You will find Me when you seek Me, if you look in earnest."

God knows the plans He has for us, and will sometimes go to extremes to accomplish it. This was proven to me on a trip into Vietnam. Myself and two others had a meeting with a lay leader of a church in a large city. We were invited to a meal with a number of key pastors in the area. During the course of the meal a young man knocked on the door and was brought to the dinner table. He stared open mouthed at myself and the other Americans with me. He excitedly began to relate his experience.

He had walked from the central highlands, a hike of several days. What he related revealed the hand of the Lord. He had been praying for Bibles and Christian literature for the churches he was responsible for. The Lord had spoken to him, and told him he must go to Saigon, and he would get Bibles. He did not believe he had really heard from God this way. So, he ignored the Word. But God had other plans for him. He struck the young pastor with a case of malaria., and the only place he could get treatment was in Saigon. Feverish and weak he began the dangerous trek through the jungle.

As he walked the Lord spoke to him again and told him where to go specifically in order to get the Bibles. It was the house we were at. The Lord told him three white people from the west would help him.

When he arrived at the clinic in Saigon, it was closed, so he decided to come to the house the Lord had told him about. When he arrived there, he met us; three white guys from the West. He was very blessed. So were we. So were all those who were eating at the table. Before the young pastor left, we prayed for him, for healing from the malaria. We loaded him down with several bags full of Bibles.

The next day our dinner host picked us up at our hotel, to take us to another appointment. We asked about the well- being of the young pastor. She related to us she had seen him earlier in the morning. He had been healed and was hiking back to his village in the highlands, rejoicing and thanking God for the miracles He provides.

THE PRICE OF REVIVAL

Matt. 5:6 Blessed are those who hunger and thirst for righteousness, for they will be filled.

I was blessed to meet with some remarkable people in a tribal area of India. This is a people who have been experiencing revival for over 25 years, as well as great persecution. I wondered how revival could be sustained for such a long time. I had a chance to meet with some of this groups intercessors. Most, but certainly not all are women. They have very busy schedules. Days for women usually begin between four and five in the morning, preparing meals for families, cleaning, then working in the fields. In the evening there are more meals to prepare, cleaning and sleep.

Because intercessors are so busy, they rise at two in the morning to meet at the church for prayer. This will last for up to three hours. It is not unusual to hear the cries and prayers of intercessors as they plead with God for their land and for revival. This is common in many of these tribal areas.

A co-worker and I spent a night in a hut church in a remote village. We were awakened early in the morning by believers who came to the church for prayer.

Is it any wonder God has blessed them with revival for so long.

Do you "hunger and thirst for righteousness?" If you don't it may be because you have become complacent in your faith walk. As the Word says, ask for a hungry and thirsty heart for the things of the Spirit. It will come to you through trials and tribulations. The blessing of revival will follow.

HEARING THE VOICE OF THE LORD

Luke 3:21,22 "When all the people were being baptized, Jesus was baptized too. and as He was praying, heaven was opened and the Holy Spirit descended on Him in bodily form like a dove. and a voice came from heaven: "You are My Son, whom I love; with you I am well pleased."

Two co-workers and I had arrived in Veradero, Cuba, on a flight from Toronto. We were standing in line with many other tourists waiting to have our passports checked and luggage inspected. A tremor of excitement shook me in spite of the oppressive heat. I watched as tourists had their luggage x-rayed, opened and contents searched. Our suitcases were full of Spanish study Bibles for pastors and Christian leaders we would be meeting. If we were caught it may not be pleasant. A friend from Canada had been arrested and jailed for this same type of activity. My turn was fast approaching. I silently prayed for the Lord to perform a miracle that would enable us to get these Bibles through for the sake of our contacts. Once again, I wanted the privilege of being an answer to someone's prayers. I had barely finished my prayer when I sensed a voice say: "Pick up your bags and go." I was stunned. I looked behind me to see a tourist checking his passport. The voice had not come from him. I obediently grabbed my bags and moved past tourists having their bags checked, and walked out of the terminal to the bus stand. Apparently my co-workers saw what I did and followed suit. In a short time, we sat on the bus taking us to our hotel, silently rejoicing at the Lord's faithfulness to our faith and action.

Have you ever heard the voice of God? Whether it's audible or in your heart, God desires to walk you through challenging times. Pray! Then move forward in faith. He will never leave you or forsake you.

THE "SACRIFICE" OF PRAYER

Matt. 4:18,19 As Jesus was walking by the Sea of Galilee, He saw two brothers, Simon called Peter and his brother Andrew. They were casting a net into the lake, for they were fishermen. "Come follow Me" Jesus said, "and I will make you fishers of men."

I have spent much travel time ministering among tribal groups in access restricted countries. I have met many people who meet this commitment to servanthood, even some who would be considered influential or wealthy and of high position. A doctor I met in a tribal area of N.E. India is such a man. By profession he is a radiologist. He was pressed into politics by people who needed his help in the political realm, against an oppressive government. It was a difficult transition for him. His desire was for medicine, but his people could be better served by his great intellect and influence being exercised as an elected official. He developed the habit of rising at 1:00 in the morning to spend three hours in prayer, Bible study and worship. This humble doctor knew a closer walk with the Lord would be his greatest tool in serving his people. He was elected to governmental office and re-elected several times in spite of much opposition from intrenched political figures. I pray politicians in our nation would be so committed.

Are you wondering if your walk is in alignment with God's plan? Ask Him to speak to your heart. His Word promises He will clearly answer you saying "Come follow Me." He will provide you with the fishing pole and bait to attract and catch many for the Kingdom of heaven.

HEAVENLY MAN

Mark 8:34 "Put aside your own pleasures and shoulder your cross (deny yourself) and follow Me."

When it comes to the concepts of servanthood and humility, the intellect will utterly fail here and brilliance has no power. Only living out Jesus' words will we ever understand His will and His way.

I met pastor Yun, a Chinese pastor and author of the best selling book: "Heavenly Man," at a missions conference in Asia. He was responsible for millions of House Church Christians in China. He has been arrested and imprisoned on a number of occasions for his Christian activities. He related how the House Church is organized and prepared to send out 100 thousand missionaries and evangelists. Their objective is to travel West from China, evangelizing, starting churches, discipling converts and spreading the Gospel all the way to the streets of Jerusalem. He shared how each one of these evangelists and missionaries have counted the cost and are willing to leave behind house, family and country, even becoming martyrs for the cause of Christ.

I wonder sometimes about the level of commitment and sacrifice the Western church is willing to make to fulfill the Great Commission? It is a sacrifice to put aside our own pleasures and shoulder the cross, (denying ourselves) and follow Jesus. But Mark 8:34 is not a suggestion, it is a command.

COUNTING THE COST OF BEING A FOLLOWER OF JESUS

Luke 18:24 "For the proud shall be humbled, but the humble shall be honored." often the cost of servanthood can be very high.

I knew of a Christian school in China. One bright school day, soldiers came and surrounded the school. Several soldiers had ropes and pulled down a large cross on top of the school. It was dragged to the entrance of the school property. The only way in or out of the property was to step on the cross. The officer in charge told the gathered students and teachers they would be allowed to go free if they stepped up, denied the Lord, step on the cross, run down the street and never return. The first student was called up. The young man saw the soldiers and their rifles. He was terrified. He denied the Lord, stepped on the cross, ran down the street and never looked back. A young woman was called up. She saw her classmate go free, so she too denied the Lord and was allowed to go free. The third student called up, another girl, looked at the soldiers, looked directly at the officer and said: "I will never deny my Jesus who died for me." The officer gave a signal and a rifle fired. Interesting! After that not one student or teacher denied their Lord. Humility and faith in action.

If you desire others to follow your example in your walk with the Lord, humble your-self, and others will be motivated to follow in humility.

CAN GOD STILL HEAL TODAY?

Mark 10:52 "Go," said Jesus "your faith has healed you." Immediately he received his sight and followed Jesus along the road.

Two co-workers and I were invited to a special church service on one of our trips to Cuba. The service was led by an old evangelist the authorities had been trying to capture for a long time. At the end of the meeting those with special needs were invited to come forward for prayer. A 17 year old girl had a huge hole in one of her teeth and couldn't get dental care. As she was prayed for, right before our eyes, her tooth was filled with a gold filling. A man who had back problems for a long time, walked with a limp because one leg was longer than the other, also wanted prayer. They had him sit in a chair. While the evangelist held his feet and prayed, the short leg grew out until it was the same length as the other. There were several such healings like this that the Lord released through his humble servant that night. What is your need today? The same Jesus who healed in the Bible still does today. We need to ask with believing prayer. Be surprised what he will do on your behalf.

Are you hoping for a miracle? So was the blind man. He was not only healed physically but spiritually, because he then followed Jesus.

POWER MANIFESTED IN WEAKNESS

2Cor. 12:9 "My power shows up best in weak people. Now I am glad to boast how weak I am, I am glad to be a living demonstration of Christs' power instead of showing off my own abilities."

I mentioned before about meeting Pastor Yun, one of China's House Church leaders. He related about a raid on a House Church meeting he was teaching in. Rather than risk capture, he jumped out of a window, three stories above the ground. His leg was broken and he was arrested and taken to prison. The Lord spoke to him to get up and walk out. He said: "Lord, my leg is broken, I can't walk." The Lord again told him to get up and walk out. Yun said when he stood up there was no pain. The Lord had healed him. He approached his cell door and it opened up before he touched it. As he came to the cell block door, he found a cart of food and coat worn by the food server. He put on the coat, knocked on the cell block door. One of the guards opened the door, saw him with the cart and let him through. He walked out of the prison doors and came to the main gate. Another guard approached him. Yun ordered the guard to open the main gate and let him out. The guard did. Yun walked out, discarded the coat and food cart and ran away.

Do you feel weak? Ask God to reveal His power in your weakness. Ask Him to let His power reveal Himself to you through signs, wonders and miracles.

THE POWER OF GOD'S WORD

Prov. 29:25 The fear of man lays a snare, but whoever trusts in the Lord is safe.

The example of David is a lesson for Christians today when it comes to submission to authorities. Taken as a whole the following scriptures reveal a spiritually mature character. No wonder he was greatly loved by God: 1Samuel 16:11-13; 18:2,5,9-14; 19:18; 24:6.

On one of our trips to Cuba we had been briefed on a secret underground printing press. I saw a tract that had been printed on this press. The Lord moved me to try and locate the people and press and try to meet some of their needs. Through contacts we were able to locate the people and press which worked overtime to try and meet the great need for Christian literature around Cuba. What a blessing to meet these humble souls, willing to risk imprisonment or worse, to print Gospel literature. They asked nothing, but we were able to provide paper, ink and finances to assist them in fulfilling the ministry God had given them. They wept at our provision for them and their press.

Are you feeling fearful? Many Christians live in fear because they do not embrace God's unconditional love for them. Ask the Lord to instill in you a complete trust in Him, and revelation of His love for you.

MIRACLES CAN COME
THROUGH FASTING

Ezra 8:23 So we fasted and implored our God for this, and He listened to our entreaty.

In 1985 the Lord led me to pray and fast on behalf of all the pastors imprisoned in the Soviet Union. How could I, a Christian living in the West begin to understand the needs or feelings of a pastor in a labor camp or prison? Through our ministry contacts I learned about the conditions these believers endured, the type of food they ate, the work they did, the loneliness of being without family and friends. The treatment they received from officials and other prisoners. At the time there were over 150 Baptist pastors in the camps and prisons throughout the Gulag. I decided to eat the same amount of bread and drink the same amount of water they ate and drank. I asked the Lord to give me insight into the heart of such a person. What about families? This had to be a great concern. With the insights came a depth of prayer for these dear ones I had never known before. I prayed for their families: That their needs be met. I prayed for supernatural strength and endurance for the work the prisoners had to do. I prayed for health in spite of the scarcity of food. I prayed the Lord grant them courage to persevere in spite of threats. I asked the Lord to visit them and reveal His love to them in loneliness. I begged the

Lord to bring them release and freedom in spite of prison bars and barbed wire. I prayed for relief in severe weather. On and on it went. In time reports started to come out through Keaston College that pastors and Christian prisoners were being released. The Lord revealed to my heart the fasting and prayers had accomplished its purpose. Over the following months of 1986 and 1987 nearly all Christian prisoners were released from labor camps, prisons and psychiatric hospitals. Did all this happen because I prayed? No! The Lord raised up Christians all over the world to pray and fast. But I had a part! The Lord blessed me through all the experiences He taught me in that time. and the prisoners were let out.

Does fasting really achieve your intended outcome? God listened to Ezra. Why would He not respond to your fasting and prayer? Try it! It worked for Ezra. It worked for me. It will work for you.

A MIRACLE LEADING TO SALVATION

Isaiah 53:5 But He was wounded for our transgressions, He was bruised for our iniquities; the chastisement for our peace was upon Him, and by His stripes we are healed.

A Chinese House Church leader shared this story with me: A House Church had been raided. The chief official mocked the believers; "Can your God fix this?" Pointing to an ugly cancerous sore on his face. The pastor stood up among the people and said the Lord would heal him, then touched the side of his face and prayed for him. That night the official felt a tingling in his face, it felt like heat. When he got up in the morning the cancerous sore was completely healed. He was able to locate some believers, shared his story and committed his life to Jesus Christ.

Do you ever pray that a physical, emotional or other affliction will go away or be healed? Consider the "healing" of the chief officer in the story. Healing wasn't just physical. There was healing of "iniquities," defined as worldly behavior. He was blessed with "peace." He was gifted with eternal life, being born again. So, when we pray for healing for someone, we want signs, wonders and miracles to touch every area of the persons life.

GOD DOES HAVE A SENSE OF HUMOR

1 Cor. 1:18 For the message of the cross is foolishness to those who are perishing, but to us who are being saved it is the power of God.

I had met Pastor John during a trip in Rangoon, Burma. He told me how he had attended a Bible conference in Florida. He had taken copious notes and was able to purchase a number of books on discipleship, which would be helpful in his ministry in Myanmar (Burma). When he returned home all his books, tapes and notes were stolen. He was very disturbed. He couldn't afford to buy another set, and even if he could, they would be confiscated in the mail. His notes couldn't be replaced. A week later he was walking past some shops and happened to see his books and tapes in the window of one of the stores. He went inside and introduced himself, but the store owner refused to give him back his belongings. He was able to purchase them back. The price was cheap. The thief had sold them for the price of some drugs. The store owner didn't think he would be able to sell material like this. After all, who would want it?

Do I really know the power in God's Word and His teachings? Neither did the store owner. Ask God to reveal the power and authority that comes from knowing His word. It will give you hope in this hopeless world.

THE BLESSING OF SENSITIVITY TO GOD'S VOICE

Proverbs 19:21 Many are the plans in a person's heart, but it is the Lord's purpose that prevails.

A co-worker and I were traveling through East Germany and Yugoslavia. As we travelled through East Germany, we saw the walls coming down. Our objective was to enter Romania where we had the name of a pastor in one of the larger cities that we were going to try and help. While in Yugoslavia we were invited to an evening Bible study group. We met a young Romanian refugee named Daniel. He invited us to stay in his apartment for the night. He told us how he had fled Romania with a hunting knife and the clothes on his back. He left his wife and daughter behind, until he could get settled in a job and living quarters. I asked him about the hunting knife. He said if he ran into any border guards it would be either them or him. We told Daniel where we were going into Romania and wanted to know if his family lived anywhere near. We had Daniel make an audio tape message to his wife and we would deliver it, and bring back a response to him.

During our time in Romania, we met Daniel's wife and child. She was shocked that two Americans would show up at her apartment with a message from her husband. She wept a great deal. She recorded a message to

Daniel. When we delivered the tape back to Daniel, he too was shocked. He told us how he had tried to get his wife out of Romania, but the government people refused. We had discussions late into the evening. The Lord blessed us with the privilege of leading Daniel to the Lord. Daniel wrote us when we returned to the States, thanking us for our gifts and our help. He said how his life had changed because of Jesus Christ. Daniel wrote how he loved the Lord and the Bible we left with him. Later, with my co-workers help from the U.S. Daniel and his family were reunited and eventually settled in the United States.

Have you prayed for someone's physical healing yet they are not healed. Maybe they even die, know that God does answer prayer. We believe the scripture that tells us, "ll things work together for good to those who love God." Trust leads to perfect answers to imperfect prayers.

HELPING MEET SPIRITUAL AND PHYSICAL NEEDS

Ps. 18:34 "You've trained me with the weapons of warfare worship; now I'll descend into battle with power to chase and conquer my foes." Passion translation

We had learned of medical needs for children's clinics, (as well as Bibles for believers) in Vietnam. We were able to get donations of medical supplies from local hospitals. We also received donations of corneas from the Lions Club eye bank, for transplanting in the eyes of children with vision problems.

Two co-workers and I loaded our equipment on a plane and flew to Bangkok, Thailand. It took several days to get the proper visas. We kept emphasizing to the authorities that we only had a few days before the corneas became useless. We had another co-worker from Bangkok who would take a large quantity of Bibles for the House Churches.

When we arrived in Saigon (now Ho Chi Minh City), The customs officials wanted to search all of our boxes of medical supplies, which were packed in plastic popcorn. Soon we had popcorn and medical supplies all over the terminal. Customs people were searching everything. With that distraction going on, our boxes of Bibles were getting through customs without being checked. Soon enough we finished up with customs, repacked our medical supplies, rented a vehicle and headed off to our hotel. Within a few days the Bibles were in the hands of believers. Some medical supplies were delivered to a children's hospital. Some of these supplies we would take to Hanoi. The corneas were successfully transplanted into young patient's eyes. We even got to observe one of the surgeries. So, the Lord provided for physical needs and spiritual needs with the Bibles we got safely in. Like David we experienced the results of our warfare worship and prayers.

Can we believe that serving the Lord will take us down the path of "warfare?" Yes, "battles" will result. If God took me through the spiritual battle with the customs officials, He will take you through the "battles" of "warfare" as you serve Him daily.

THE POWER OF
INTERCESSORY PRAYER

Psalm 75:9,10 "But I will proclaim the victory of the God of Jacob. My melodies of praise will make Him known. My praise will break the powers of wickedness while the righteous will be promoted and become powerful."

Another pastor and I were invited to a tribal area of N.E. India to minister in what they called "Revival Hour." Thousands of people would attend this event. It was a time of prayer, repentance and healing. We were able to visit the grounds where the event would go on, lasting for three days, with two or three services a day, beginning early in the morning and lasting until late at night.

On our first visit I noticed a hut where there was loud praying and weeping going on. I asked one of our tribal pastors what was going on. He said: "Those are the intercessors. They have been here for a month preparing the spiritual atmosphere for the Revival Hour. I was thinking this event was going to be a powerful time.

The first service began by the intercessors leaving their hut and joining us on the platform. There was such an incredible presence of God on these dear prayer warriors as they climbed the stairs to their seats on the platform, I was stunned. I had never experienced a holy presence like I did at that time. All I could do was weep. I wasn't the only one. Others on the platform and many in the vast sea of people also began to weep. After a time of prayer and worship that lasted well over an hour my pastor friend brought the first message. There was a move of the presence of God. All over the grounds of that meeting place, people wept and cried in repentance. The ground in front of the platform began to turn to mud because of the people's tears. The prayer time was a mighty move of God as so many lives were touched. O that we could see a move like this in America.

I was blessed to bring a message during the "revival hour." Again, God moved mightily on the people. There was not enough room for all the people who came forward and filled the area in front of the platform. Chairs had to be moved out in order to accommodate all those who came forward for prayer.

Your "melodies of praise" WILL break the powers of wickedness, so the righteous will be promoted. Keep seeking God. Don't stop. He answered the intercessors in N.E. India. He will answer you.

GOD'S TIMING LEADS TO MIRACLES

Psalm 5:3 "At each and every sunrise you will hear my voice as I prepare my sacrifice of prayer to you. Every morning, I lay out the pieces of my life on the altar and wait for your fire to fall upon my heart."

Three co-workers and I had flown to Bangkok, Thailand. We were going to meet up with another team of couriers to carry Bibles into the communist country of Lao. Christians were being greatly persecuted. They were discriminated in work, some jailed or imprisoned, some were even killed for their faith. In spite of their hardships, they still prayed for their need for Bibles. We wanted to be an answer to their prayers.

We were informed by the ministry director, when the other team arrived from Vietnam, we would all be involved in briefing, given our Bibles to carry into Lao, pray together, and get to know each other. The next day we found out the other team was delayed in Vietnam. So, our group was briefed, given boxes of Bibles and told we would meet the other team before we flew out the next morning. They would have the names and locations of our contacts. The next morning, we learned the group had not yet arrived but would meet us at the airport. Our bags were packed with Bibles and the few clothes we would need for our stay in Lao. We taxied to the airport, got checked in and waited for the other team to show up. We discussed and prayed about what we should do if the other group didn't show up. We decided to go ahead and board, fly into the unknown and trust the Lord to lead us. Soon we had to get on the plane not knowing who our contacts were or where they were located. As we settled in our seats with the other passengers, I was praying for the Lord's direction. The flight attendant was closing the cabin door. We heard some pounding on the door. The attendant opened the door and I saw the other group come on the plane. I knew the team leader, and when she walked by my seat, we gave each other a nod. I was greatly relieved. The Lord was doing a work to increase our faith. Soon He was taking us safely through customs with all of our Bibles, which were delivered into the hands of our contacts.

Are you desperate for the Lord to intervene in your circumstances? So was I. God often tests our faith by making us wait for His help. Faith building comes in waiting. Keep waiting. Keep trusting.

THE POWER OF PRAISE FROM CHILDREN AND INFANTS

Psalm 8:2 Through the praises of children and infants you have established a stronghold against your enemies, to silence the foe and the avenger.

My co-workers and I were visiting a Christian school we helped finance. It was located in a tribal area of the Himalayas. When we entered a classroom, the little children, about nine and ten years old, were quiet, not running around, not talking or misbehaving. It amazed me! The teacher wasn't in the room, having been called to another room. What would happen in a classroom in the States with no adult supervision in the classroom? When the teacher returned, she spoke to the students. They stood up by their desks and began to sing a worship song. What a magnificent sight and sound. Some of the students were so touched by the song, tears ran down their cheeks. These young children, had come from Buddhist and Animist backgrounds. Their parents wanted them to get a good education because the government schools were considered poor. These students came to the school, learned about Jesus, accepted Him into their lives, then shared with their parents. The adults saw the changes in the lives of their children. Most of them too, committed their lives to Jesus Christ. In this way the entire region was being transformed from Buddhist to Christian. Now we can see the truth of Psalm 8:2.

Our Lord hears the praises of "children and infants." If the faith of children and infants can be the vehicle used by the Lord to change hearts in others, why can it not be used by you to touch the hearts of your family? Keep praying with that child-like trust.

THE BLESSING OF AMERICAN MISSIONARIES

2Tim. 3:12 "and indeed, all who desire to live godly in Christ Jesus will be persecuted."

Paul and Silas' response was to pray, sing and praise. God's response was to send an earthquake, perform a miracle of opening prison doors, breaking off chains. When the prisoners could have escaped, they remained. The presence and power of God was so great, they wanted to hear more. Then a warden and his family were all brought into relationship with Christ and baptized.

We brought our friends from a tribal area of the Himalayas to America for a visit. It was their first time here. So many of the things we have here was overwhelming for them. The interstates with big semi-trucks, all kinds of cars were a sight to see. The orderliness of our driving. Grocery stores that were packed full with so much variety in food.

They were able to visit a large amusement park with the rides, all kinds of junk food to eat. What surprised me was their comments about the people, so many were obese.

I was able to get them on a Christian radio station to do an interview. They were intimidated by all the sound equipment and microphones. but when we got deeper in the interview, and they shared about the challenges they face and the persecution they experienced because of their faith, I knew it would be a challenge for the listeners. We do not yet go through the hardships and even martyrdom that is a part of their lives. By the way, THEY were very thankful for America. It was missionaries from the U.S. that first brought the Gospel to them.

If your material things, home, car or job were forcibly taken away because of your faith, would you accept it as a blessing to be "persecuted?" Serving Jesus has a price. Pray for strength to persevere despite persecution that may come your way.

GOD CAN MAKE SEEING EYES BLIND

Micah 3:8 "On the other hand I am filled with power – with the Holy Spirit of the Lord – and with justice and courage to make known (declare, praise) to Jacob (God's people) his rebellious act, even to Israel his sin." NASB

We never know what to expect when crossing a border into a restricted country, loaded with "contraband" Bibles for needy believers. At times we are able to go through customs with little or no searches of our luggage. Other times our luggage can be searched. our Bibles discovered, and then the questioning begins: "Why are you bringing these books into our country? Who are you taking these Bibles to? Don't you know this is illegal?" On and on it goes. I've been detained, had Bibles confiscated, even been arrested. Never kept very long before being released. If caught, the Bibles are taken away to be destroyed or sold on the black market.

We always pray before crossing a border. It is usually something like this: "Lord, when you were here on earth you made blind eyes to see. Now you have to make seeing eyes blind. We have precious cargo of Your Word for those who have none." It is our rule, if caught, to never lie, but we will NEVER give up our contacts.

I have seen God work so many miracles over the decades. I never stop being amazed at how God enables His Word to reach His people in need. Over the years of this blog, I have shared a number of stories, and will continue to do so.

On my first trip to China, so long ago, I was with a tour group, most of whom were carrying Bibles. The customs officials were so overwhelmed with so many tourists going in at one time, they were hurrying us through with only cursory checks of our luggage or none at all. We were able to quietly celebrate God's goodness to us AND those who would receive such needed Bibles.

Do you believe that Jesus can and will heal the blind? Can He also make seeing eyes blind? The Lord gives us what we need in the moment.

THE AUTHORITY OF GOD'S WORD

Psalm 149: 5-9 "Let the Godly exult in glory; let them sing for joy on their beds." (NASB) "God's high and holy praises will fill their mouths, for their shouted praises are their weapons of war! These warring weapons will bring vengeance on every opposing force and every resistant power – to bind kings with chains and rulers with iron shackles. Praise filled warriors will enforce the judgement doom decreed against their enemies. This is the glorious honor He gives His Godly ones. Hallelujah! Praise the Lord!" (PT)

As a co-worker and I drove through Europe on our way to Romania, we saw evidence of the people rejecting communism to embrace democracy. We saw the wall coming down between the two Germanys. Ahead of us lie the Romanian border. This country was untouched by the Democracy movement. We were blessed getting through the border with barely a cursory search and few questions. Our objective was Bucharest to meet a pastor who had spent much time in prison. He was also an outspoken critic of the government run by dictator Nicolae Ceaucescu. Romania was a very restricted country. In our briefing we were told to avoid the pastors house if we saw a government vehicle parked in the street near his house. When we arrived, the government vehicle was there. We were unable to make contact with this dear brother in the Lord.

We had been invited to share in a church service, which we gladly did. After the service we met with about 150 pastors from around the country. In the course of the meeting, I asked about the freedom movement occurring in other formerly communist countries. They were pleased, but as a group they said it would never happen in Romania as long as Ceaucescu was in power. I sensed the Lord moving on me. I raised my voice and declared the words from the Psalm that opened this blog. I said loudly: "Ceaucescu will be brought down. We will claim this verse. We make it our prayer. Our praise will move God's hand to defeat the enemy, just as it did for Israel. Let us agree together to pray, worship and intercede until we see Romania free.

After prayer we hugged the pastors and we began our trip back to Holland. Soon after we left, there was an uprising. Hundreds of women tried to march on the presidential palace but were turned back by the army. The next day thousands of men and women marched to the presidents residence. The army had orders to shoot the protestors. Many, many people were cut down like wheat being harvested with a sickle. But the protests didn't stop. Eventually the peoples uprising was successful. Ceaucscu's government collapsed. On Christmas Day of 1989 I saw Nicolae Ceaucescu and his wife executed. This was seen on t.v's across the world.

Does this not show the power of praise and prayer? 2nd Chronicles 20 is a powerful example of the power of praise declaring the Word of God in spiritual warfare. I encourage you to search it out and read it.

Do you feel you're beyond God's willingness to respond to your prayers? He is just as concerned about your needs as the needs of nations. "The prayer of faith" will bind those powers of darkness that are trying to hinder your relationship with Him.

PERSEVERING IN THE FACE OF MARTYRDOM

Rev. 5:8 and when He had taken the book, the four living creatures fell down before the Lamb, having each one a harp and golden bowls of incense, which are the prayers of the saints. (NASB)

We had conducted a healing festival in a tribal area of Central Asia. We had seen God touch many lives with healings, deliverances and salvations. We always face threats from radical Hindus and Buddhists. When our time in the area was completed, we returned to the States. We found out soon afterward, right after we left, radical Hindus came to the home of our translator, broke into his home, took this dear man of God outside and proceeded to beat him to death. His wife and children fled to safety before they could be injured or killed.

When we found out about our friend's martyrdom, we sent resources to his wife and family. They were able to start a small business which met their needs. The family is doing well in spite of the loss of their father and husband. He wasn't the first friend and co-worker to be martyred for his faith, and he won't be the last. But we press on to accomplish the will of God with praise and prayer.

We pray expectantly before every trip: for our protection and the protection of those we work with. "The prayers of the saints are recorded in the heavenly realm. We must trust with faith and thanksgiving for answering according to His perfect will.

THE PURPOSE IN SUFFERING

Eph. 6:11 Put on God's complete set of armor...so that you will be protected as you fight against the evil strategies of the accuser.

We were conducting a healing festival in a remote area of the Himalayas. Travel is long, hard and dangerous in this part of the world. We arrived worn out but excited for the ministry that lie ahead of us. We usually do two meetings a day. One reason is the time it takes to pray for and tend to the needs of those who come to these meetings. Some people travel for days on foot to attend and be prayed for. After the first service a man and his daughter shared about their experience in coming to the Lord. The man and his wife were sleeping. The wife was very ill with incurable cancer. Their daughter was in another room sleeping. The man and his wife were awakened by a bright light that began to glow in their room. A man could be seen in the light who began to speak to them. He told them to turn from worshipping idols to the true and living God. After a while the image and light disappeared. They called for their daughter to come quickly. They told her about the light and the man in the light. When they described the man, she ran back to her room and brought back a book with a picture of what an artists interpretation of what Jesus looked like and showed her parents. They said excitedly that it was the man who spoke to them. They prayed and asked Jesus to save them and lead them.

The man's wife passed away the next day. The father and daughter heard about the healing festival and came to get instruction and share their testimony. That night after the meeting the father and daughter returned home to find radical Hindu's in their home waiting for them. They had knives and swords and proceeded to kill the father. The daughter escaped and returned to the festival grounds. Some believers took her in and protected her.

We followed up on this young woman for the next few years. After training she became a teacher in a Christian school. Today she has a family of her own. She could truly teach us much about spiritual warfare.

Our prayers cause the devil to retaliate! He tries to wear us down to get us to give up. I have personally felt the dark effects of Satan's interference when I pray and plan a work of God. Don't let discouragement keep you from getting to your destination.

THE HARVEST IS GREAT BUT THE LABORERS ARE FEW

Psalm 51:15 "Lord God, unlock my lips and I will overcome with my joyous praise." (PT) Psalm 55:17 "Every morning I will explain my need to Him (The Lord). Every morning, I will move my soul toward Him. Every waking hour I will worship only Him and He will hear and respond to my cry." (PT)

We were invited to teach in an underground Bible school in a S.E. Asian country. The young men who attended this school came from various tribal groups in this country. They learned farming skills to help them when they returned to their villages. They learned English in which all the classes were taught in. They were also grounded in extensive Bible teaching and church history. These students had to make a two-year commitment in order to attend the school. They were eager students you could tell desired to be immersed in the Word of God. It was a blessing to be a part of their education.

While in this country we attended night markets. So many products were sold at these places. We picked up many souvenirs for friends and family back home. What impressed us most was all the young people who came to the markets. They weren't there to buy products, but to meet other young people. Some of our team thought it would be wonderful to arrange a Christian concert that would attract and impact the young people. Along with the music there would be a sharing of the Gospel. We were very excited about this concept. Until we discussed it with our pastor contact in the country. He said: "Yes, it could be done, but be prepared to go to jail. It would be illegal and the authorities would not look kindly on it." That definitely dampened the enthusiasm for a concert outreach. Currently in this country there is much persecution of Christians. We were told stories of pastors and prominent believers just disappearing. Right now the best outreach is one-on-one sharing the Good News.

To have this kind of "commitment " a person must "every morning" seek the Lord. "Every morning" give your soul to the Lord. We want to experience a full commitment to God.

COUNTING THE COST OF
SERVICE FOR GOD

Luke 10:3 "Go your way, behold, I Am sending you as lambs in the midst of wolves.

Would you have committed your life to Christ if you knew what it would cost? Persecution, discrimination, being an outcast from family and friends, even martyrdom? I wonder about the great faith of the apostle Paul. The Lord showed him how much he would have to suffer for the cause of Christ. In spite of this, he pressed on in obedience. So like brothers and sisters in Christ we have worked with over the many years.

We had a team of couriers who were trained and willing to accept the consequences of being detained in an access restricted country. What were they trained for, and what would lead them to be detained? We were making multiple trips into a restricted country in S.E. Asia with Bibles for persecuted Christians. Most of the Christians we worked with have experienced discrimination because of their faith. Some experienced jail or prison. and we know of those who paid the ultimate price. Martyrdom! They still pray and cry out for the Word of God, which is in such short supply. Our team of couriers believe Christians have a right to own a copy of the scriptures if they choose. It is hard for us in America to identify with those who do not have Christian book stores, and quite often no church to attend. Some will meet secretly in small house groups. Others may not have this opportunity, so they worship alone or with family. The pressure to compromise is strong. But having worked with believers living in these conditions for many decades, I see their faith is very great. Thus, we will not give up our efforts to get the Word of God into restricted areas.

In the country we were ministering in, there is genuine revival. Many non-believers are being witnessed to by these courageous Christians and committing their lives to Christ.

Have you given up anything to follow Jesus? Lose family, abandoned by friends, negative treatment on your job? Jesus tells us to serve like a lamb among wolves. Sound dangerous? So is carrying The Word of God into restricted countries. Let's count the cost, and serve Him.

HOW BIG OF A BIBLE COULD YOU BUILD FROM MEMORY

Psalm 119:11" I have stored up Your Word in my heart, that I might not son against you."

How do we measure success in our culture? Someone who has the best, the most, the largest of something, whether in business, education, work environment, or whatever, is considered successful.

Those who work with us don't measure success by the number of Bibles which can be safely delivered in a restricted country, or how many times we can get through a border without being caught. We measure success by the spiritual growth taking place in our lives, that is not dependent on our circumstances.

Would you consider it a success or failure if you were detained at a border, all your Bibles are confiscated, but the next day you lead the desk clerk at your hotel into a relationship with Jesus Christ? He had never heard this truth before, because he lives and works in a communist country.

The people we minister to in restricted countries don't always have access to much in the way of scriptures. When they do, they will memorize it. I have to wonder, if all our Bibles, Christian books, tracts, scripture portions were taken away, how big of a Bible could we build from memory?

Great question! How BIG of a Bible could we build from memory? Believers in restricted countries know the power of God's Word. What will it take for us who live in non-restricted countries to recognize the power of the Word?

WHAT IS THE GREATEST GIFT?

Mark 16:18 "They will pick up snakes with their hands; and when they drink poison, it will not hurt them at all. They will place their hands on sick people, and they will get well."

We were able to develop a relationship with pastors in Cuba. We not only provided them with study Bibles and teaching materials they needed but could not obtain in their country, we also provided food we purchased from diplomatic stores, which Cubans are not allowed to purchase from. Our friends were always overwhelmed and appreciative. We learned that there are many restrictions placed on pastors and believers. To step outside these rules puts our friends in a position of punishment. For example: A pastor is not allowed to visit the home of one of his sick congregants unless he has government permission. Imagine if that took place on our nation.

On a visit to one of our pastor friends, it was not a good day! The family was very upset. Their 17 year old son was going to be taken away from them to do one year of forced labor in the sugar cane fields. We prayed much over the boy and his family, for their protection and strength to endure all that he would go through. We prayed his faith would impact the lives of those he had to labor with.

A year later on another trip to the island, we visited with the family. The son had been returned and survived the ordeal and was a courageous witness. I am so thankful for this family and others like them we have met and worked with over the years. Their example of perseverance should be a lesson for us all.

Are you willing to risk the consequence of publicly displaying your faith? God's miraculous power in manifested by bold faith. Let us be willing to live like Christians in the New Testament.

THE SACRIFICE OF GROWING NEARER TO GOD

2Tim. 2:3; 3:12 "Suffer hardships with me, as a good soldier of Christ Jesus. and indeed, all who desire to live godly in Christ Jesus will be persecuted."

Is it possible that a person could make a mistake concerning their abandonment to the Lord? One may abandon themselves to the Lord hoping and expecting to always be loved and spiritual blessed by Him. If you have given yourself to the Lord during some pleasant season, please note: You cannot suddenly turn back around and take back your life at another season...when you are being crucified.

Some co-workers and I were invited to do some leadership training for pastors in remote N.E. India. Our guests were tribal pastors from Burma (Myanmar). These pastors had to make their way to the Indian border. They were covertly brought across the border to where we had transportation to bring them to where the training would take place. Many of them walked for days through dangerous jungle to reach the border. The danger wasn't just animals, but Burmese military who would shoot them or imprison them. We heard so many horrific stories of the persecution tribal believers suffered. One example we heard often: Soldiers coming into a village and trying to force Christians to reject Jesus and return to Buddhism.

Those who refused could be shot. One pastor told us he was concerned about his fellow believers, who out of fear would turn away from the Lord. We were told by these courageous pastors that very few gave in to the threats of the military. My friends and I were there to bring greater insights into the Word of God. But I must say we learned more from them about standing strong in the storm of persecution.

WHO SAYS GOD CAN'T HEAL TODAY

Jer. 17:14 "Heal me, O Lord, and I shall be healed; save me and I shall be saved, for you are my praise."

We were finishing up some ministry in a S.E. Asian restricted country, making preparations to return to the U.S. We found out the son of one of our key contacts, who heads an underground Bible school, was seriously injured in a motor cycle accident. He was a passenger when the motor cycle was struck by a truck. The young man operating the cycle was killed. The pastor's son was in the hospital in a coma, and not expected to live. We stopped at the hospital on our way to the airport to visit the family and pray for the boy. The parents of the boy were very distraught, but we encouraged them then prayed for the boy. As we left we committed to continue to pray for the young man.

We found out about a week later the young man was awake and responsive. Doctors said he would have brain damage and not be normal again. Soon after we heard he had been released from the hospital and doing very good. Some months later we were back in this country for more ministry. We met the young man and his family, the boy who doctors said wouldn't live and even if he did would have brain damage. He was doing well, going to school and playing soccer. We rejoiced together at the greatness of our God and his healing and restoring power.

God answers our prayers! Sometimes miraculously, which touches lives beyond our expectations. the Bible calls these "signs, wonders and miracles." We also expect God to do spiritual healing to follow physical healing.

THE IMPACT OF STANDING
FIRM IN THE FAITH

Psalm 23:4 "Even though I go through the darkest valley, I fear no danger, for you are with me; your rod and your staff they comfort me."

The Lord wants to meet with us in our time of suffering. He is able to manifest Himself to us in the midst of our greatest need.

We met with Pastor Dimitri from Romania in his little apartment. He shared this story with me. This was during the time when Romania was still under a communist dictatorship and was trying to crush Christianity. He had been arrested on one occasion. The authorities wanted to know about those in his underground church. they also wanted to know about his contacts with Westerners. He would not give them the information they desired. So, they beat and tortured him. Still, he would not give them the information they desired. So, they put him in a cell with no windows and nothing else in the cell, not even a bucket. For a time, he prayed for his family and his fellow believers. Then he began to worship the Lord.

During the night he heard the sound of metal scraping against the cement wall. Dimitri knew what the guards were doing. They were going to release huge, hungry rats who because of their numbers would overcome him, kill him and eat him. It had happened to other prisoners.

When he heard the sound of the rapidly approaching rats, he cried out to the Lord and repeated: "Jesus, Jesus!" A light began to glow in the cell, which got brighter and brighter. Dimitri knew the Lord was appearing to be with him. The Light was so bright it froze the rats and they were unable to attack Dimitri any further. He was able to kill every one of the rats and pile them in a corner.

The next day the guards opened his cell door, planning on removing his half -eaten corpse. But there Dimitri stood, healthy and untouched by the rats. the guards yelled: "Who are you? What kind of man are you?" They were shocked and amazed. Dimitri told them he was a minister of the True and Living God and they needed to surrender their lives to Him. Their response was to quickly usher him out of the prison before something bad happened to them.

Are you facing your own "dark valley" right now? Is danger lurking? So too with Pastor Dimitri. God's Word doesn't say we will not face "dark valleys." It does promise "comfort" during your season of suffering.

THE IMPACT OF ONE MAN'S RELATIONSHIP WITH GOD

Luke 14:27 "Whoever does not bear his own cross and come after me cannot be my disciple.

Based on the experience of the last 40 years, it is hard for us in America to understand and identify what it is like to be a believer in a restricted country. How can we comprehend having to meet as believers secretly maybe in someone's home, in a jungle setting, in a cave, on a deserted ocean beach, in a sugar cane plantation. Why is that? We don't have to be concerned about being arrested, jailed, tortured, imprisoned, placed in a labor camp, or even killed because of our faith in the Lord Jesus Christ. What? No comfortable climate-controlled church building with a coffee bar, large screen, padded pews or chairs. No sound system or light show to capture our attention to worship the true and Living God? We don't have to fear police or military busting up our service, hauling away the pastor and church leaders in handcuffs, beating them as they take them away. Imagine no Christian book stores. Possibly no Bibles at all. Maybe no New Testaments. Maybe not even a page or two from a Bible. We don't have to fear being kicked out of our families, shunned by friends and others in our community.

Talk about sacrifice and the way of the Cross. On two different occasions in two separate countries, I was invited to teach in home meetings, packed out with believers eager to hear what I had to share. Both times I had local men standing right next to me during my teaching time. Both times I asked the pastor what these men were doing. They told me if the police broke into the room and started shooting these men were to throw me to the ground and cover me with their own bodies. I wept at such willingness to sacrifice oneself for a stranger.

Why is it when the Apostle Paul told us: "All who desire to live Godly in Christ Jesus WILL be persecuted," and we are not? Is it because we are too fearful to be those believers who fulfill the Great Commission because we don't want to offend anyone, or cause anyone to think we are judging them, or make them uncomfortable with the Truth of the Gospel? Most of these things I share with you I have seen and experienced first-hand. Believers who do not live in America EXPECT to be persecuted. One believer from a restricted country told us: "It is the way of the cross," when it comes to suffering and hardship for the Name of Christ. Like apostle Paul, are we living out of our salvation from day to day, and can we say as believers we are crucified daily and are no longer responsive to the world and its temptations?

Is the Lord asking you to carry a cross today? Health, family, financial burdens, or one of many other crosses? Jesus says to "bear it" and follow Him. I encourage you to ask the Lord for strength. Then you will fulfill His plan for your life.

DO OTHERS SEE GOD WORKING THROUGH YOU?

Philip. 3:8-10 "Yet indeed I count all things loss for the excellence of the knowledge of Jesus Christ my Lord, for whom I have suffered the loss of all things, and count them as rubbish, that I may gain Christ and be found in Him, not having my own righteousness, which is from the law, but that which is through faith in Christ, the righteousness which is from God by faith; that I may know Him and the power of His resurrection, and the fellowship of His sufferings, being conformed to His death."

We met a Christian business woman in a S.E. Asian restricted country. We were there to provide Bibles for the underground Church. Through her business she provides jobs for many people. The proceeds of her success helps underground pastors and churches. If the government was aware of her work to help persecuted Christians, her business would be closed and she would be jailed. But she courageously carries on. We were able to spend time with her and meet her employees, observe their work, and purchase products to bring back to the States.

Madam Fute reminds me of Dorcas who is mentioned on Acts chapter 9:36-43. She was raised from the dead by the apostle Peter. She was known for being a friend and helper of the poor. Dorcas was also a woman of wealth AND an influential Christian. People in this S.E.

Asian country could SEE the Lord through the life and work of Madam Fute.

Have you lost family, friends, health, or things because of your faith? Consider it all joy, for Jesus gives us His replacement …which is peace and rest in the midst of suffering.

Printed in the USA
CPSIA information can be obtained
at www.ICGtesting.com
CBHW020520240624
10480CB00004B/13

9 781958 892527